SELL YOUR

STORY TO

HOLLYWOOD

WRITER'S POCKET GUIDE TO THE
BUSINESS OF SHOW BUSINESS

Kenneth Atchity

STORY MERCHANT BOOKS · LOS ANGELES · 2016

Sell Your Story to Hollywood:

Writer's Pocket Guide to the Business of Show Business

www.kenatchity.blogspot.com

ISBN: 978-0-9969908-7-5

Story Merchant Books
400 S. Burnside Ave. #11B
Los Angeles, CA 90036
www.storymerchantbooks.com

Interior Design: Lisa Cerasoli & Danielle Canfield

Cover Design: Dafeenah Jamal, www.IndieDesignz.com

SELL YOUR
ST(TO)RY
HOLLYWOOD

Kenneth Atchity

PREFACE

IN THE OLD days, as far back as ten years ago, you wrote a book, published it through an agent with a traditional publisher, then the agent helped secure a film deal for your book. If you were among the fortunate authors whose books were made into movies, that was the conventional scenario. But we're not living in traditional times. Through the expanding influence of the Internet and the changes in both publishing and entertainment it's all gotten more complicated, more eccentric, and more exciting.

This little book aims to help you figure out how to get your story told on big screens or small. It's *not* going to give you rules and regulations, because they simply don't exist today. Any rule I could promulgate has and will be broken. That said, visit Appendix D for "13 Rules for Breaking into the Business" (from my earlier book, *A Writer's Time;* e-book: *Write: Time*). What I'm offering you here, instead, is nearly thirty years of observation of *how things happen* in show business, the business of entertainment (better known around the world as "Hollywood") [**Ed. Note:** *for definition of words that appear in quotes the first time they're used consult the Hollywood Jargon section of industry terms at the end*].

My Hollywood experience ranges from writing, to managing writers, to producing their movies for television and theaters. I've seen the Hollywood story market from nearly every angle, including legal and business affairs.

I spent my first career as a professor, a career I embarked upon innocently because I wanted to focus my efforts on *understanding stories* and *helping writers get their stories told*—and here I am thirty years later still pursuing the same goal. You can take the professor out of the classroom, but you can't take the classroom out of the professor.

I've made films based on nonfiction books, like *The Kennedy Detail* (nominated for an Emmy), and deals for a number of nonfiction stories like *The Magic Castle, Ripley's Believe-It-or-Not! The Columbia Malignancy, Mrs. Kennedy and Me, Sante: The Kenneth Kimes Story, Sex in the South, Higher Ground,* and *Nobody Walks.* But most of my experience lies in turning novels into films. The process is much the same for both, so whenever possible I'll use the word "book" to mean "novel" or "nonfiction" (never, please, "nonfiction novel").

As a lifelong story merchant, what I develop and sell are "stories." Stories rule the world. Many of the observations outlined in this book are simply about *selling stories to Hollywood.*

Everyone in today's attention-challenged world likes lists so I chose to use them often in this book. But don't let that lead you to think that *if I just do each thing on the list, I can't fail.* Of course you can fail! This is show business! There are thousands of ways to fail in show business, just as there is in the world of inventions, stock market brokering, or neurochemistry. The good news is there are *many ways to succeed,* too. Every movie that gets made has something unique in its development history. Remember, show business is a business where there are no hard and fast rules. That's what screenwriter William Goldman, in his wonderful book *Adventures in the Screen Trade,* meant when he said that the only rule in Hollywood is that *nobody knows anything.*

All films that have made it to the screen share one quality: someone behind the film's making was persistent.

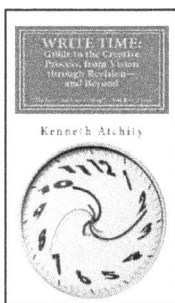

In my first book for writers, *A Writer's Time: A Guide to the Creative Process from Vision through Revision—and Beyond* (e-book: *Write: Time*) I wrote that, in Hollywood, four things guarantee success, in this order:

- Perseverance (or determination or stamina)

- Connections

- "Being fun to work with"

- Talent

And that the only one of them not *sufficient* in itself for success is talent. There are plenty of talented people making their way to L.A. each year, but only if they have at least one of the other three elements will they succeed. Thirty years have passed since I wrote that, so I'd like to add one more element: luck. Luck happens—or not. If not, then you need three things: (1) knowledge of how Hollywood works, (2) persistence and (3) a plan. This guide is dedicated to helping you with all three.

Keep in mind Winston Churchill's eloquent exhortation to the British people during World War II: *"Never give up, never give up, never give up."*

When people make you wonder what your odds of success are, tell them: "The odds don't apply to me."

I truly hope this pocket guide expedites the transformation of your show business dreams into realities.

You can watch my web presentation *Sell Your Story to Hollywood at* http://realfasthollywooddeal.com/

Sell Your Story to Hollywood

1 | The Conveyor Belt

IMAGINE A CONVEYOR belt in the sky that carries every story that's headed for the screen. Your goal is to somehow get your story from the back of the belt, where "naked stories" lie, to the very front of the belt where fully-clothed stories are about to leap into "principal photography."

What do the stories at the "stardust point" of the conveyor belt look like? At the very least, they have

1. A perfected script that has been vetted numerous times by dozens of highly-critical technical and creative industry readers, and rewritten accordingly. It's not unusual for a script to have gone through twenty or more revisions.

2. A finalized (and "bonded"!) budget that has undergone even more revisions than the script.

3. A "start date" agreed upon by all parties to the filming.

4. A location that works for the best interests of the film.

5. A solid legal foundation that provides contracts for everything from the "underlying rights" to the services to be provided by every member of the cast and every member of the crew.

6. A director who understands the story enough to "enhance the flame" created by the screenwriter (who enhanced the flame the original storyteller created), and who the financers and "completion bond" executives trust to deliver a completed film.

7. A committed cast suitable not only to the script, but also to the distributors, sales agents, and finance representatives.

8. An international sales agent who has agreed with the producers on selling the completed film to every possible market.

9. A "domestic distributor" who has shown interest in distributing the film in the United States and Canada.

By contrast, stories at the far end of the conveyor belt lack any or all of these elements, the *farthest* from stardust being, in this approximate order:

- a "great idea for a film,"

- a written "pitch,"
- a book (fiction or nonfiction),
- other source material (like a magazine article, or life rights),
- a "treatment,"
- a stage play, or first draft screenplay.

They aren't ready to be filmed until they gather all the other necessary elements.

One of the nearly infinite "Catch 22s" of show business is that every story on the conveyor belt risks being leapfrogged over by a story that has more of the necessary elements. No wonder it takes forever to make a film. I recently got a film into production that we'd been working on for twenty years. It sold to networks twice, but always got stopped along the way by "regime change" or "policy change."

But first you have to *get on that conveyor belt*. This book aims to help you figure out not only how to get on the conveyor belt but how to keep advancing.

2 | The Easy Way to the Screen

THE FASTEST PROGRESS to the screen I've ever experienced was with John Scott Shepherd's *Joe Somebody*. Exactly three months, to the day, after Fox 2000 decided to make the film, I received a call from our production exec there, Carla Hacken. "The good news," she said, "is that your film goes into 'prep' tomorrow." "What's the bad news?" I asked. "You won't recognize it when the new writers are through with it." I gulped. The studio had hired new writers to insert some broader humor for the star Tim Allen.

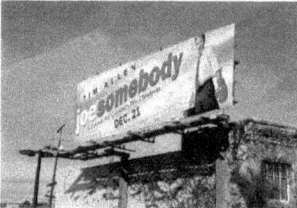

All else being equal here's all you have to do to get your book made into a film:

1. Turn your book into an Internet sensation, to draw the attention of "trackers" who are on the constant lookout for new stories to turn into films. Trackers are paid to track stories! They find out who controls the rights and,

once they do, report back to the producer or studio bosses who've retained them. More than ever, studios and indie producers are scouring the web for stories that stand out in one way or the other. If you can get your book to rank high on Amazon and/or iBooks, you're much more likely to have it noticed by Hollywood. Research key review blogs like The Millions, called by the New York Times, "the indispensable literary site," and blogs like Nancy Pearl's Book Lust podcast (airs on NPR's *Morning Edition*), Maureen Corrigan's reviews on *Fresh Air*, and Tom Lutz's on *Los Angeles Review of Books* podcasts on KCRW.

2. Make your book into a major bestseller. Do whatever is necessary to get it to appear on bestseller lists, especially that of the *New York Times*. Studios and indie companies alike gravitate toward books that have been bestsellers because it gives them comfort in knowing that a story has a "pre-sold audience."

3. Get your book favorably reviewed by *New York Times, The Washington Post, The New Yorker, The Wall Street Journal, People* magazine, as well as *Publishers Weekly, Library Journal, Booklist*. These influential trade journals are read by publishing insiders: newspaper and magazine editors, bookstore and library book-buyers, literary agents, and film industry trackers and execs looking to get the jump on the next great movie or television project.

Sometimes a great review can overcome unremarkable sales and get your book noticed by people who make decisions about potential film projects. I get a call or two a week from trackers, and it warms my heart to know I live in a jungle where stories are important enough to be hunted down.

4. Bring your book to the attention of a major director, or a "star," preferably over lunch or a drink—which you're buying. If you know a filmmaker personally, this is no time to be shy. Pitch your story to them wherever you can—at the supermarket or the carwash, at an NBA game, in church. If they're intrigued, they will ask to read it; they certainly won't hesitate. If they're not interested, they'll say something polite like "send it to my agent, please," and might at least offer you some direction that can be useful.

5. Find one of the top agents in Hollywood who handles books and convince him to represent yours to show business. If you don't have personal access to an agent, the list of these agents is easy to find in directories like Jeff Herman's *Guide to Book Publishers, Editors & Literary Agents,* the *Writer's Market Guide to Getting Published,* or *The Hollywood Creative Directory.* The *Hollywood Screenwriting Directory* boasts over 4,000 industry listings, and includes examples of formats, "query" letters, treatments, and loglines. It's even easier to find agents and managers on the Internet at sites

like www.literaryagencies.com and www.literarymarketplace.com. Look up how the agent likes to be approached and follow those instructions precisely. Or you can meet them in person at writers' conferences like the Writers League of Texas Agents & Editors or the Hollywood Pitch Festival.

6. Write, or hire someone to write, a professional treatment of your novel, following the guidelines presented in my (and co-writer Chi-Li Wong's) *Writing Treatments That Sell.* Then, after registering it with the Writers Guild of America, http://www.wgawregistry.org/registration.asp, use your treatment to query agents, producers, directors, etc., as mentioned above—first sending a brief "logline" to find out if they're interested. *Life or Something Like It*: An ambitious and self-involved reporter is sparked into action to try and change the pattern of her life after she interviews a psychic, who tells her that her life is meaningless and she's going to die—soon.

7. Convince or pay a professional screenwriter to write a screenplay of your book. This takes a huge step toward getting your film made, because no film can be made until there's a screenplay—and producers hate to pay for screenplays. But it must be a *great* screenplay so be careful who you choose for this. Having a bad screenplay is *much worse* than having no screenplay at all. In extremely rare cases, the author (you!) can write the screenplay yourself

but a great screenplay by this method is the exception rather than the rule—because authors generally lack the professional expertise and know-how required to construct a shootable script.

8. Bump into a billionaire to develop and finance a movie based on your book, starting with the business plan, script, and budget and including securing "equity" to cover at least twenty-five percent of the film's budget. In other words, do it yourself—become a producer/filmmaker who believes in his or her story strongly enough to do whatever is necessary to get it to the screen. That is how writers often succeed in today's booming independent film business. It's how Sophocles and Aristophanes got their plays performed at major festivals, and why so many of Shakespeare's plays survive after first playing at the Globe Theatre—which *he* managed.

If you have any of the above and don't know what to do next, reach out for help.

But it's an imperfect life, where more miracles are created than happen by themselves. I'm reminded of the story of the guy who kept saying, "God will sell my house." He never did move. When he got to heaven, he said, "I had faith you'd come through for me and sell my house." God replied, "And I had high hopes you'd put up a For Sale sign."

Assist in making your own miracle! Though they've been known to happen, the situations listed above are very unlikely for most new writers. All else is *never* equal. The simple truth is that most books never make it to the screen.

3 | Why Books Fail to Make It to the Screen

THE SLOWEST PROGRESS to film I've experienced, so far, is the twenty years I mentioned. That's how long we pushed to get *A Christmas Journey* by Rexanne Becnel made into *Angels in the Snow*. Here's a list of handicaps that keep books from being movies drawn from my own experience and that of the execs and interns who've worked for me over the years, and from the experiences of the agents, managers, execs, financers, distributors, directors, and producers I've had the great pleasure of knowing and chatting with:

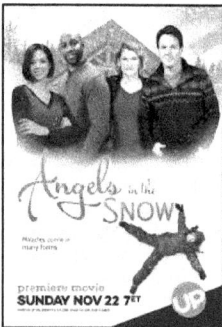

1. The book is neither a notable bestseller *nor* has great reviews, though it's still a great story waiting for its recognition.

2. The author gave no thought to the requirements of *drama*. Sometimes a filmmaker

(screenwriter or director) with vision can remedy this. But you have to attract that person first.

3.   The decision-makers are not picking up the book and reading it. Reading takes time. Authors seeking representation complain that none of their books have been made into films. At any given moment, we in Hollywood have literally stacks of books on our desks in Los Angeles—from New York agents and publishers, and novelists around the world. But as we go through them to find the ones that might make good motion pictures or television movies, we're constantly running into the same issues.

In that mysterious place called the story department, where story editors read three to five or more scripts or books a day and provide "coverage" for them, most often the project is passed over in favor of a book that fulfills the dramatic needs of commercial movies. The sad thing is most likely you will never see the coverage of your story—that's a proprietary in-house document strictly for the use of those who make acquisition decisions. See Appendix C for a sample coverage from one of my companies.

Here are the most frequent "story editors'" complaints:

"It's not clear until page 200 who the 'protagonist' is."

Make sure you introduce your protagonist memorably at the very beginning. When a star's management or agency reads for him or her, if they don't see their client's character introduced in the first two pages, they don't have the patience to go searching for the character the producers want their client to play. The protagonist can be male or female, but it must be a character with whom the audience will immediately identify. In the opening pages of *Lethal Weapon,* Mel Gibson's character, Martin Riggs, is introduced when he begins his morning with a piss, a swig of beer, and a game of Russian roulette—with his handgun in his mouth. Who can resist watching a *suicidal homicide detective?* In the opening scene of the series *Orphan Black,* Sarah Manning is introduced watching herself walk in front of a metro train.

Keep the story focused on the characters that are integral to telling it.

"I can't relate to anyone in the book."

Whether the main character is sympathetic or not, he or she must be so intriguing and relatable that you can't stop watching what happens to him or her. When Shakespeare's Richard III comes on stage to face us at the beginning of the play or film and tells us the evils he plans to inflict on the royal court, we can't tear our eyes away from him:

GLOUCESTER

Now is the winter of our discontent
Made glorious summer by this sun of York;
And all the clouds that lower'd upon our house

In the deep bosom of the ocean buried.
Now are our brows bound with victorious wreaths;
Our bruised arms hung up for monuments;
Our stern alarums chang'd to merry meetings,
Our dreadful marches to delightful measures.
Grim-visag'd war hath smooth'd his wrinkled front;
And now, instead of mounting barbed steeds
To fright the souls of fearful adversaries,
He capers nimbly in a lady's chamber
To the lascivious pleasing of a lute.
But I, that am not shaped for sportive tricks,
Nor made to court an amorous looking-glass;
I, that am rudely stamp'd, and want love's majesty
To strut before a wanton, ambling nymph;
I, that am curtail'd of this fair proportion,
Cheated of feature by dissembling nature,
Deform'd, unfinish'd, sent before my time
Into this breathing world, scarce half made up,—
And that so lamely and unfashionable
That dogs bark at me as I halt by them;
Why, I, in this weak piping time of peace,
Have no delight to pass away the time,
Unless to spy my shadow in the sun
And descant on mine own deformity:
And therefore, since I cannot prove a lover,
To entertain these fair well-spoken days,
I am determined to prove a villain
And hate the idle pleasures of these days.
Plots have I laid, inductions dangerous,
By drunken prophecies, libels and dreams,
To set my brother Clarence and the king
In deadly hate the one against the other:
And if King Edward be as true and just
As I am subtle, false and treacherous,
This day should Clarence closely be mew'd up,
About a prophecy, which says that G

Of Edward's heirs the murderer shall be.
Dive, thoughts, down to my soul:
When studio execs say they can't relate to anyone, it usually means the lead isn't a strong male character. To maximize your chances for success in

Hollywood, give us a strong (preferably male) lead in your novel who, good or bad, is eminently relatable—and who's in the "star age" of 35-55 where at any given moment twenty male stars reside—a star being a name that can get a film financed by his mere attachment to it. Guys like:

Matt Damon
Brad Pitt
Denzel Washington
Idris Elba
Bradley Cooper
Leonardo DiCaprio
Will Smith
Robert Downey Jr.
Dwayne Johnson
Hugh Jackman
Jackie Chan
Channing Tatum
Chris Pratt
Matthew McConaughey

Ben Affleck

Chris Hemsworth

The reason for the male preference isn't sexist, it's financial: Women viewers, old and young, determine not only box office success but also television success. They are the driving force behind ticket sales and Nielsen ratings. Women want, for the most part, to see strong male leads. That's what probably draws them to the box office, and to a new series or film on television. The "Ulmer Scale" is used by sales agents and distributors to rate stars by their box office earnings and popularity. It's from this listing that the term "A-lister" became current in the industry.

Of course female leads make good films that attract women, too, and a few female stars—Julia Roberts, Sandra Bullock, Halle Berry, Jennifer Lopez, Meryl Streep— even get a film financed. But to increase your odds for major success, go with a male lead because that's what the biggest market share demands.

Nothing is simple in this life, not even Hollywood. *Life or Something Like It,* starring Angelina Jolie, didn't do that well because women aren't rushing to take their husbands or boyfriends to watch a

15

man fall in love with the sizzling Jolie. And the director, Stephen Herek, insisting on her having platinum hair only sealed the results.

"At the end, the antagonist lays out the entire plot to the protagonist."

Make sure you don't neatly "wrap up" your plot with *explanation* or *summary* instead of action, breaking the dramatic rule of "show, don't tell." *Telling* us what happened to get to this particular ending is intrinsically undramatic, and therefore a sure way to weaken your story's chances of reaching the screen. Much better to sprinkle the clues that make the plot come together throughout the story, interweaving them with action turning points so the audience figures it out as they watch the story unfold. Watch *The Usual Suspects* or *Chinatown* as great examples of doing this interweaving effectively.

"There's no real pacing."

A book that is a good candidate for being made into a movie is one that offers a rollercoaster ride of unpredictable and gripping twists and turns, like *Avatar* or *Terminator III: Rise of the Machines*.

You can help insure this by structuring each of your three "acts" into three acts, and each scene into three acts: compelling beginning, unpredictable middle, and conclusive, satisfying ending.

In *Writing Treatments That Sell* (e-book: *Write: Treatments*), Chi-Li Wong and I offer a simple way to chart the pacing of your story (the "Intensity Rating"). You can use this diagnostically to chart the pacing of a story you've already drafted; or you can use it to plan your story. Either way, here's what you do:

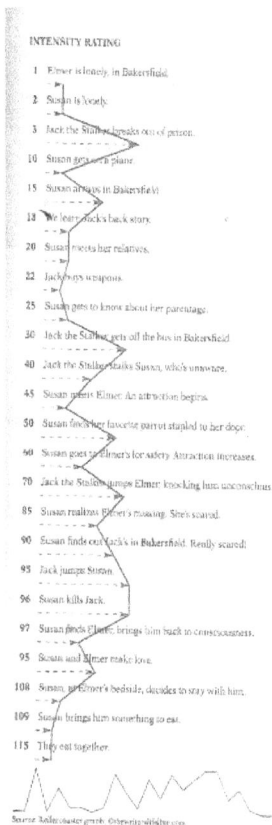

INTENSITY RATING

1   Elmer is lonely, in Bakersfield.

2   Susan is lonely.

3   Jack the Stalker breaks out of prison.

10   Susan gets on a plane.

15   Susan arrives in Bakersfield.

13   We learn Jack's back story.

20   Susan meets her relatives.

22   Jack buys weapons.

25   Susan gets to know about her parentage.

30   Jack the Stalker gets off the bus in Bakersfield.

40   Jack the Stalker stalks Susan, who's unaware.

45   Susan meets Elmer: An attraction begins.

50   Susan finds her favorite parrot stapled to her door.

60   Susan goes to Elmer's for safety. Attraction increases.

70   Jack the Stalker jumps Elmer, knocking him unconscious.

85   Susan realizes Elmer's missing. She's scared.

90   Susan finds out Jack's in Bakersfield. Really scared!

93   Jack jumps Susan.

96   Susan kills Jack.

97   Susan finds Elmer, brings him back to consciousness.

95   Susan and Elmer make love.

108   Susan, at Elmer's bedside, decides to stay with him.

109   Susan brings him something to eat.

115   They eat together.

Source: Rollercoaster graph, Rollercoasterpublishers.com

17

- On a single sheet of paper, as in the accompanying illustration, write 1 (for "page 1") in the top left-hand corner, and 115 (p. 115) at the bottom left-hand corner. Then start filling in the most important scenes of your action line with a single line to describe each scene in the story, like "Elmer is lonely, in Bakersfield."

- Beneath that line, type one to ten hyphens (n-dashes) to indicate the intensity of drama in that scene. The last hyphen in any line should be an arrow. It's best to write the scenes down from memory, on the principle that if you don't remember them they aren't obligatory to include in your overview.

- Once you've done that for every scene, turn the sheet of paper sideways and draw a line from the tip of each arrow to the tip of the next arrow. What you will see is a graph of your story's action, which allows you at a glance to make adjustments to make sure the audience remains on a "wild ride" all the way to the end.

"The characters all sound the same."

When I was in graduate school, the exam questions I enjoyed the most were those that made us identify a story by a single piece of dialogue. I learned then what this meant: "dialogue must fit character," and I delighted in identifying Falstaff, Iago, Achilles, Aeneas, Sancho Panza, Ishmael in

Moby Dick, and Tom Jones from their characteristic speech. This is a high standard to hold yourself to, and not even all great authors achieve it; but it's a good way to get the attention of Hollywood readers immediately. A closely-related comment:

"There's no dialogue, so we don't know what the character sounds like."

Express your characters' personalities in dialogue that distinguishes them from one another, which will compel an actor to see themselves playing the role. In *Whiskey Tango Foxtrot*, when war correspondent Kim Baker (played by Tina Fey) begs General Hollanek (Billie Bob Thornton) for something quotable that will give her readers an insight into the horrors of war, he says: "War is like fucking a gorilla. You keep going until the gorilla wants to stop." In one line, we get a glimpse not only into the character's cynicism but also into the irrational darkness of war that Baker has been entangled in.

One of the sure reasons for a "pass" from the story editor is the observation that, "the characters all sound the same." If a character is well-constructed, she will express herself characteristically, meaning that no one else in the book will sound exactly like her.

Of course you can trust your screenwriter to create the dialogue for you, but studio shelves are filled with screenplays that never get made into films because even the screenwriters weren't able to bring the dialogue alive—any more than the novelist did. Don't leave that as a possible outcome. Write powerful, active dialogue. One of my favorite examples is from Ernest Hemingway's short story, "Hills like White Elephants":

> "Would you do something for me now?"
>
> "I'd do anything for you."
>
> "Would you please please please please please please stop talking?"
>
> He did not say anything but looked at the bags against the wall of the station. There were labels on them from all the hotels where they had spent nights.
>
> "But I want you to," he said, "I don't care anything about it."
>
> "I'll scream," said the girl.

Drama is action, and dramatic action comes in two colors: (1) action (He rings the doorbell. The door explodes from a shotgun blast. He staggers to his knees.) and (2) dialogue that moves the story forward like the lines from Hemingway's story, or these from Robert Towne's *Chinatown*:

EVELYN

She's my daughter.

Gittes slaps her.

GITTES

I said I want the truth.

> EVELYN
>
> She's my sister.

He slaps her again.

> EVELYN
>
> She's my daughter.

He slaps her again.

> EVELYN
>
> My sister, my daughter.

He slaps her again.

> GITTES
>
> I said I want the truth.
>
> EVELYN
>
> She's my sister and my daughter.

Ideally you'd structure your novel as much around action and forceful dialogue as around ambience and reflection. That just makes the best storytelling.

"There's not enough action."

This complaint is obviously closely akin to the "pacing" comment. Internal monologue, thinking, reflection, description, observation, contemplation—none of those novelistic elements translate well to film. The screenwriter must find a way to transform them into something we can see or hear or both. Instead of eight paragraphs of contemplation, *telling* the reader what a character is thinking, *show* the character walking along a shoreline, hands in pockets, head bent in thought.

"There's nothing new here. The concept has been used to death."

That's a tough comment to hear, and I hope you never do. What it usually means is that the story-teller is out of touch with the way things are, unaware that his or her story offers nothing new on an all-too-familiar subject. Entertainment professionals recognize that there are no truly original ideas. All of us are stimulated by the same events and it's par for the course to see similar story ideas in development at the same time. At the end of the day it's about your unique POV or take on an idea and the details of your execution. Consider the originality of Spike Lee's *Chi-Raq* (based on Aristophanes' *Lysistrata*), *10 Things I Hate about You* (from *Taming of the Shrew*), *Pretty Woman* (*Pygmalion* + Cinderella), or Karl Sutter's *Sons of Anarchy* (heavily influenced by *Hamlet*).

"The protagonist is reactive instead of proactive."

According to classical Greek drama, the *protagonist* literally means the "first actor," the primary cause of the drama. Make sure your protagonist takes charge of the action that shapes his or her destiny, instead of being the passive victim of events. Just as no one likes eternal victims in real life, no one has sympathy for them in fiction. They are simply boring. We want characters that actively get into and out of trouble. The old Hollywood formula remains true:

Act 1: Get your hero into a tree.

Act 2: Shake the tree.

Act 3: Get your hero out of the tree.

This works for comedy OR tragedy. The hero either gets down safely, or falls on his or her head. He falls because of his own misjudgment, not external forces.

"At the end of the day, I have no idea what this story is *about*. There's no 'high concept.'"

In chapter five I'll talk about "high concept" in detail. This comment means that the story editor can't figure how to pitch what your story's about in a single sentence. It's a giant-killer comment that usually stops further consideration of the book in the "acquisitions meeting." If the story editor is fumbling to explain the story, he's liable to hear "Next!"

Another way to explain this is *simplicity,* as Michael Hauge (author of *The Hero's Two Stories*) puts it. If your story isn't simple enough to pitch easily, it's in trouble. People like a story they can easily wrap their heads around.

Ken Kesey's *One Flew over the Cuckoo's Nest* was made into a film because the question, "What's the story about?" is easily answered: It's about an inmate in an asylum who's saner than his keepers. William Wharton's *Birdy* is about a boy who believes he is a bird.

The buyer needs to be *hooked* by your "logline": "It's a fish out of water—only she's a mermaid" (*Splash*).

If you *can't* reduce your novel to one line, it's probably *not* a good candidate for film. The logline gives the movie's "premise" at a glance: "Overwhelming ambition leads to self-destruction" is the logline of *Macbeth* as well as of *Death of a Salesman*.

For studio films, the only non-"franchise" stories that have much of a chance are high-concept ones like *Weekend in Las Vegas* or *American Sniper*—where the title automatically markets the picture: You know what you're going to see at the theater.

"The main character is 80, and speaks only Latvian."

I tried for years to "set up" a favorite novel of mine, in which the main character was eighty. By far the hardest resistance came from practical producers worried that an eighty-year-old actor would be un-bondable, which means the budget of the film relies on the protagonist's continued good health. By the same token, if your protagonist speaks a language spoken only by a fraction of the world's population, you can expect to run into massive resistance from all but the most philanthropic financers. I'm not saying either situation is impossible. I'm just saying it's going to be more impossible than most stories.

"It's set in Papago…in the 1960s, and is filled with long passages in Uto-Aztecan."

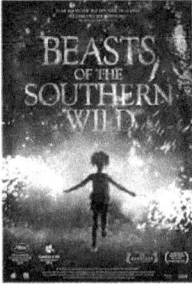

Hollywood is prejudiced against setting stories in a foreign land that doesn't have a direct appeal and tie-in to the American audience. That's why they made Paula Hawkins' *Girl on a Train* in New York instead of London, where the novel is set. Suffice it to say that successful American movies are almost always set in America. That's even why the rest of the world buys them—they like to see what happens here, whether it's the weirdly non-mainstream world of *Beasts of the Southern Wild* or the mainstream zaniness of *The Wolf of Wall Street*. As much as the world might hate our politics from time to time, global audiences love American subjects and American action. Stories set in other countries may be made in other countries, but they're all too rarely made—or even distributed— in America. If foreign-set stories win an Oscar nomination, they may then be distributed mini- mally in the US.

The foreign market is in love with American stars and with Hollywood production quality because it has set the visual standard. So a movie has got to have either an American lead, or at least be set in

America to have a really good chance. *The Bourne Identity* films are the obvious exception because the ongoing story, rooted in America, is set all over the world. But there's generally an American dimension and the lead is American. If you want the odds to be in your favor, set your story in the United States. Yearly we receive numerous books to be considered for film that are set in South America with no American leads. If the books are by major authors, they might eventually get produced as indie films in the US; but it can take years. *Love in the Time of Cholera* by Gabriel Garcia-Marquez, one of the greatest novels written in the last century, finally got made into a movie that did not do it justice—and did not do good business at the box office. It didn't help that the leads were old at the story's "climax."

"There are no set pieces that make it a movie."

Producers call it "opening the story up." Stories that are mostly interior are more challenging than stories like *Avatar, The Perfect Storm, Life of Pi,* or *Captain Phillips,* that take the audience to a setting that screams to be a *movie—moving pictures* in a world we want to experience with our eyes. Remember, film is first and foremost a visual medium.

If you must have a conversation occupying the larger part of a chapter, *take it outside* to someplace interesting. Create an atmosphere that directors itch to capture on camera.

"There's no third act…it just trickles out."

Make it clear that there are three acts in your story. Oddly enough, most book writers don't think that way. A successful movie *has* to think that way because it must be dramatic in order to hold an audience's attention from first to last. The big problem with most novels is that they always have act one, and then some big turning point happens that takes you into act two—but often there's no act three. The story just keeps going and going until the end, which often feels tacked on.

This can easily be remedied at the drawing board, or in retrospect when you edit your first draft, by asking, "What is the twist at the end of the book that makes the third act even more riveting and compelling than the second act was?"

If the novel doesn't have a clear-cut act three, a screenwriter is brought in whose job it is to clarify act one, two and three and make sure that they register strongly as such in the audience's mind. Make sure a dramatist looking at your book will clearly see three well-defined acts: act one (the "setup"), act two ("rhythmic development,"

"rising and falling action"), and act three (climax leading to a conclusive ending).

"Acquisition editors" for the traditional publishing houses aren't as set on the three-act structure as they should be. A novel can be so engrossing in the world it creates that editors figure readers won't care as much about the traditional beginning, middle, and end.

When it comes to films, though, the proven formula is just the opposite. Inconclusive third acts lead to box office and ratings disappointment. And if you follow that dramatic formula, which is as old as Aristotle's *Poetics,* you'll end up creating a better novel too. All readers like stories they can follow.

"There are way too many characters."

How many characters do you really need to tell your story effectively? Do the pruning yourself, even before the screenwriter gets his hands on your story. Cut the characters that aren't recurring and/or absolutely necessary to tell the story powerfully. The pain it causes you to do this trimming is why authors aren't normally the best choice to write the screenplays for their own stories. They have a hard time letting go of the characters they've come to know and love.

"The whole thing is overly contrived."

Contrivance means that you simply don't believe the action. It's too far-fetched, not grounded in reality, or not unfolding through the laws of cause and effect which govern convincing drama. The moment a storyteller loses credibility with the audience, he's lost his audience. Make sure that every event in your story is constructed to avoid that accusation. People love to leave the theater and, over drinks, poke holes in a story. The good storyteller fills those holes at the drawing board.

"I can't relate to anyone in the book." Or: "We don't know who to root for."

That comment usually means there's no clear and "sympathetic" protagonist, no one the audience can root for— which translates

Ken with Jim Belushi at the premier of *Joe Somebody*.

to mean, "We'll never find a star to play this role." Whether the main character is sympathetic or not, he or she must be intriguing and relatable so much so that you can't stop watching what happens to her or him. We meet Tom Ripley wearing a Princeton blazer. Because of the false identity the blazer suggests, wealthy Herbert Greenleaf offers Tom a handsome payment to go to Europe to convince his own son, Dickie, to come home. When Tom meets a wealthy heiress, he pretends to be Dickie—and the snowball of deceit proceeds downhill. Why do we care for him? Because the story becomes an object lesson for what might happen if we allowed our lower nature to take over our actions.

Of course anyone with the mind of a researcher can list a film or two that got made despite one or more of these story editors' objections. But for novelists who are frustrated at not getting their books made into films that should be small consolation and is, practically speaking, a useless observation. Yes, you might get lucky and find a famous Bulgarian director who's fascinated with the angst of octogenarians, studied pacing with John Sales or Jim Jarmusch, and loves ambiguous endings. But we're planning to make a business out of this not just sell a single show, right?

Back to our list:

Though I've observed the phenomena for several decades now, it still surprises me that even best-selling novelists, even the ones who complain that no one has made a film from their books yet, don't write novels dramatic enough to lend themselves easily to mainstream film. To compound the problem, it's a well-known phenomenon in to-day's publishing that, with very few exceptions, the more books a novelist sells the less critical his publisher's editors are of his work. So time and again we read novels that start out well, roar along to the halfway point, and then peter off into bogs of formless character development or action res-olution. Moral of this story: just because the book was edited by a publisher doesn't mean it's appro-priate for making into a film.

1. A publisher invests between $25,000 and $100,000 or more in publishing your book. A low-budget feature film from a major Hollywood studio today costs at least $50 million. There is, from a business point of view, *no* comparison. Risking $50 million means the critical factor is raised as high as can be imagined when your book hits the "story department"—much higher than the critical factor of even the finest publishers. Hollywood *studies* what audiences want by logging, in box office dollars, and through surveys, what they respond best to. On top of that, development costs are higher than ever, diminishing the chances that a company will take on a book where they might jump at a screenplay. It takes artistry, experience, and time to create a solid screenplay from a solid book, and even more so if the book is a great story idea but not so solid in the storytelling. When you're spending millions and millions on a film you want to make sure the structure it's built on, the *story,* is as perfect as it can be.

2. Accordingly, if you really want to add film to your profit centers as a novelist, it would behoove you to study what makes films work. Disdaining Hollywood may be a fashionable defense for writers who haven't gotten either rich or famous from it, but it's not productive to furthering your cinematic career. Before you plan your next book, sit down and watch

ten successful movies in a row. I once outlined *Jaws* just to understand exactly what was happening minute by minute, page by page (one page normally equals one minute of running time). I learned how tightly structured this horror thriller was, and how cleverly anticipation foreshadowed the first actual appearance of the monster. Todd Klick's *Beat by Beat* is a minute-by-minute analysis of what *must be* on each page of a screenplay. It's a real eye-opener to novelists that have never experienced, or even imagined, the kind of mechanical precision screenwriting requires.

4 | Write Your Own Treatment

NO MATTER WHAT problems your book might display when it comes to making it a candidate for the screen, they can be remedied with a good "treatment."

What is a motion picture treatment? Think of it as a roadmap to what the audience will see and hear on the screen. Chi-Li Wong and I define the treatment in *Writing Treatments That Sell* (e-book: *Write: Treatments)* as:

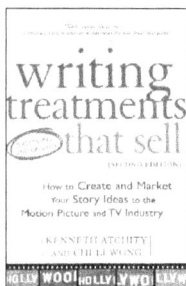

> ...*a relatively brief, loosely narrative, written pitch of a story intended for production as a film for theatrical exhibition or television broadcast. Written in user-friendly, dramatic but straightforward and highly visual prose, in the present tense, the treatment highlights in broad strokes your story's hook, primary characters, acts and action line, setting, point of view, and most dramatic scenes and turning points.*

When you write your treatment, pay attention to what filmmakers require to allow them to create compelling and successful films, and modify elements in your book that will cause story editors to recommend a pass. That way you'll give your story a fighting chance to be considered seriously for translation to the film.

In industry practice, the treatment has two complementary functions.

First, it's diagnostic, helping the storyteller identify what works and what doesn't work without the time and psychological investment of writing the screenplay.

Second, it's a great marketing tool for showing your story to potential allies in Hollywood in a way that indicates its film potential.

Start by reviewing the ingredients of some highly successful films so you can introduce or reshape your novel in your treatment:

1. Contemporary. Period movies (set before 2000) are much more challenging to get made than contemporary ones. So when you're transforming your story, ask yourself this question: Can I set this story TODAY? That will give your story much less resistance from the story department.

2. Male lead, if possible, in the star age-range of 35-55. Make your story eminently *castable*.

3. Make sure your protagonist is clearly defined and sympathetic—a protagonist with a dark problem.

4. The thing that makes your protagonist sympathetic is *clear and relatable motivation.* We must understand why he needs to do what needs to be done to escape from his dilemma. I discuss building character and motivation in Chapter Five of *A Writer's Time* (e-book: *Write: Time*).

5. Make sure your antagonist is as clearly defined, sympathetic, and powerful as your protagonist—with a worthy goal. It's a rule of Hollywood that the "stronger the villain, the stronger the hero." An antagonist with no dimensions, no interior conflict, is cardboard and makes your film feel like a comic book.

6. Make sure that both protagonist and antagonist have a "character arc" that's clear in the treatment. Audiences want to see a major character evolve from one position to another quite different one. An example, from *Delivery Man,* is Vince Vaughn's character: he starts out as the last guy on earth who should be married or have kids; and ends up being an involved father to 533 kids, and proposing to his girlfriend, who gives birth to another of his children. A character that evolves compels us to invest in his emotions; that's what's meant by being "sympathetic." We suffer along with him.

7. Clearly define your story's three acts, and make sure its ending is satisfyingly *conclusive*. Not an ambiguous ending, and not a tragic ending. Very few movies that you go to the box office to see have a tragic ending. But, there are exceptions and some of the exceptions almost prove the rule. My favorite exception is *Witness,* a classic romantic thriller. In the last scenes of *Witness*, we see the hard-edged Philadelphia detective John Book (played by Harrison Ford) falling in love with the innocent Amish handmaiden Rachel Lapp (played by Kelly McGillis) on a Pennsylvania farm. We're rooting for them to stay together because their love is so sweet and unusual. They seem to be soul mates. In the final scene of the movie as Book leaves, director Peter Weir uses a very long shot of Book driving away because, as the two lovers part when the detective decides to return to Philadelphia, the audience's heart is breaking. His car moves very slowly as though he was thinking it over. Halfway down the road, we're rooting for him to make a U-turn and come back to stay with her forever on the Amish farm—even though we don't really believe in our hearts that would make any sense. Their cultures are just too different. So, in the second half of the slow drive as he continues to the highway, we're now giving up that fantasy because we realize it doesn't work. And as he turns right and enters the highway and leaves forever we know that was the right ending—

and then we feel this big rush of anguish as we admit the world is not always romantic. *Witness* is one of the very few movies that manage to have an unhappy ending by traditional definition, but a right ending doing honor to the romance. Not every romance is forever, and that's what this movie is saying. Some romances are what they are when they are; they don't have to be eternal to be valid. But normally what audiences crave most is a happy ending. We're getting plenty of unhappiness in our daily lives. We want the runaway bride to finally stop running and get married.

8. Throughout the treatment, focus on the *scenes*, making sure that each illustrates *conflict*, the engine that drives drama. If there's no conflict in a scene, cut the scene. There's no need to write transitions between the scenes. Just start a new paragraph to get to the next one.

If you write your book to include these elements in the first place, everyone who reads it will think and say, "This should be a film." That's the very thing we're wishing for!

Think of a treatment as an uninhibited letter to a friend describing your most dramatic experience. Minimum "syntax"; all action. Nothing extraneous! Write it in the present tense, and write only the *scenes*, the units of drama. Include only the "obligatory action," the key dramatic scenes. These are the scenes without which the story makes no sense. Focus on the conflict between protagonist and antagonist, and make sure you track the over-all arc of the story. Leave most of the details out. They don't belong in your treatment—save them for the script.

Here is a sample of what a treatment might look like—one by Joe Eszterhas (*Sliver, Flashdance, Basic Instinct*), that despite its tiny flaws, sold for millions of dollars:

ONE-NIGHT STAND

He meets a woman in a hotel, and his and his family's life will never be the same.

Idea by Joe Eszterhas

(Directed by Adrian Lyne)

Jack Ramsey is 35 – smart, glib, good-looking. He is at a convention of public relations people in Boca Raton, Florida at the Boca Beach Club. He works for a small agency in Syracuse, New York. He is married and has two children.

The convention has just ended. He is sitting at the bar of the Beach Club with a couple of his friends, drinking. His plane leaves in four hours. His friends leave and he is left at the bar alone. He sees a beautiful young woman sitting at a table in the bar glancing at him. He checks his watch, then goes over to her. He offers to buy her a drink.

Her name is Karen Anderson. She's 27. She's been here for the convention too. She's from San Francisco. He buys her a drink. They talk, they laugh. They like each other. He keeps checking his watch. She notices. He tells her his plane is leaving soon. He hasn't even checked out yet. They look at each other. You could fly out to tomorrow, she says. I could, he says. Why don't you? She says.

They are two strangers. He takes her to his room. He tells her the truth: He's married, he got kids – this is nothing but a one-night stand. She smiles; she doesn't object.

His room faces the sea. They talk, they make love, they eat, they drink... all night long. As the night goes on, as they get to know each other better and better, they tell each other about their loves. She tells him it's clear to her how unhappy he is. She says he's chosen a kind of spiritual death for himself because of his children. He is taken by her life force, by her sense of freedom.

She lives the way she wants to live. She is alive. You do this all the time, don't you? She asks. A piece of ass here, a piece of ass there— a stranger to talk to here and there. What kind of life is this—this life of one-night stands?

Our focus as they stay in this room all night is microcosmic. Their initial clumsiness with each other... the million tiny hesitations that lead to bed... the initial nervousness of their love-making... the way they eat their sandwiches naked in bed. Their talk about sex is honest, startling—there is no need for false compliments.

He calls his wife from his room, tells [sic] he is coming in tomorrow, not today, tells her he loves her, talks to his kids—and as he talks to his wife and his kids, he fondles Karen, makes love to her with his hands.

As the night goes on, we see they care more and more about each other. What about you? He is led to ask her. Is this enough for you? What about a commitment instead of the one-night stands? She's never met the right person, she says. She has needs... that she needs... to satisfy.

At one point, they fall asleep, curled in each other's arms. He wakes to hear her on the phone—her girlfriend's going to pick her up at the airport, she says. She and Jack argue, too, during the course of this night—he's into responsibility, she's into freedom. Their arguments have a humorous edge—they like each other, we see, but they like fighting each other too, teasing, trying to bust each other.

It's morning. She says she has to check out and get to the airport. We could stay another night, he says. We could both fly out tomorrow. She smiles, Why don't we do that? she says. I'll go down on you while you call you wife to tell her. It's a joke—she has to go.

If you're ever in San Francisco and feel like a one-night stand... she writes her phone number down... they kiss for the last time... put another notch in your belt, she says, another piece of ass in your memory... call me. She gives him her phone number. She smiles.

He leaves for Syracuse the same day. His wife and kids pick him up at the airport. He is the perfect suburban husband and father. We hear his empty lies about the convention, we see him playing with the kids, we see him in the bedroom with his wife, claiming he's tired...

His wife wants to make love to him and he does. But it's Karen who's in his head. As he makes love to his wife, he sees flashes of himself making love to Karen. When they are finished, his wife holds him and says: I missed you so much, Jack. He says, I missed you too. I really did.

We see him briefly at the office. One of the friends we saw him with at the Boca Beach Club bar teases him about probably scoring some pussy after they left. He doesn't appreciate the joke. He is off-center. Something is wrong. He can't get Karen out of his head. She's moved him in a way he never expected. His wife sees something is wrong too, asks him. He says there's nothing wrong. He plays with his kids. We see tears welling in his eyes.

Late at night at the office, he gets Karen's phone number out of his wallet. He stares at it a long beat and then, almost against his will, he calls her. The number she has left him in San Francisco is not a working number. We see him making calls, desperate to locate her in San Francisco. He calls the agency she told him she works for–they have never heard of a Karen Anderson. He doesn't know what to do, desperate to find her—and then he remembers the phone call she made from his hotel room. He finds his hotel bill, looks through the numbers called from his room.

He finds one, circles it. It is a local call made in Boca Raton. He calls the number. She answers the phone. Karen, he says. Don't ever call me again, she says and hangs up. He tries to call back. The phone is off the hook.

He tells his wife he has to go to a meeting with a client in Miami. She can tell something is very wrong. You were just there, she says, why didn't you see him when you were there? It just came up suddenly, he says. She drives him to the airport with the kids. We see the strain between them as he tries to make idle chit chat, pretending it's just a business trip.

He goes to a private detective in Miami and says he needs an address for the phone number he has. That's it? the private eye laughs. That's easy. He has the address after one phone call. It costs Jack $300.

He drives out to the address. It's in Coconut Grove, a Miami suburb an hour freeway drive from Boca Beach Club. It is a suburban neighborhood, a ranch style house with a Volvo and a Toyota in the driveway. He watches the house from the car... and sees her. She is with a 5-year-old little boy and a man in his mid 30s. They look like the perfect suburban couple. They look like he and his wife do with their kid. He stares, shattered.

She sees him watching them from the car. There is blind panic in her eyes that she tries to hide from the man with her. She goes into the house with the man and the child. A little later, the man gets into the Volvo and leaves.

He keeps sitting in the car, watching her house. She comes out, looking scared, comes to his car. Not here, please, she says. I can't talk here. Where? he says. At the bar at the Boca Beach Club at seven o'clock. It is the place where they first met.

43

He sits in the bar, drinking, checking his watch. Seven. Seven-fifteen. Seven-thirty. She comes in finally—she looks gorgeous—she wears the same dress that she wore when she first met him here. She sits down. He tells her he's in love with her. She tells him it's impossible. She's married. She's got her little boy. It was just a one-night stand.

She tells him how she does it. She goes to hotels where conventions are being held when her husband is out of town on business. Her husband is probably doing the same thing, she smiles. What about all the things she said about freedom, about spiritual death? It's a fantasy, she says. It's the way I'd like to be. There is no Karen Anderson, she says. My name is Susan Watkins.

He stares at her shattered. They look at each other. I don't have to be back until eleven, she says quietly. He takes her up to his room. They make love again. She whispers, I love you when she comes. She gets up, puts her clothes on, and walks out of the room without ever looking at him again.

His wife and kids pick him up at the airport in Syracuse. How was your meeting? His wife asks. Great, he says, I couldn't wait to get home. He smiles. It is a joyous smile. It is the saddest smile in the world.

That night, we see him in bed with his wife. She is asleep. He stares at the ceiling. He gets up and checks the kids. He looks at them a long beat, and then he goes downstairs to the kitchen. He picks up the phone and dials a number. She picks the phone up in Coconut Grove. Susan, he says. A beat, and she says—Yes. Hi, he says, it's me. A beat, and she says—Hi. She smiles. It is a joyous smile. It is the saddest smile in the world.

IF YOU'RE TRULY angling for the pot of gold, start dealing with reality.

The studios today are producing, for the most part, two kinds of films. One type is pre-established franchises (comic books, TV series, famous novels, toys, such as *Star Wars, Captain America,* and *The Hunger Games.* The other type is *high-concept scripts* that are either conceived of "in-house" by executives, producers, managers, and agents who know what the market responds to—or by "spec" screenwriters determined to break the bank.

Writing even the greatest screenplay that isn't high concept is choosing either the indie path or sheer self-indulgence.

Dealing with "high concept" is one of the most challenging and frustrating tasks of the Hollywood writer, agent, or producer; reducing the story to a compelling logline is what high concept is all about. As a former academic not prepared for a world focused on marketing, it took me years to realize that the term "high concept" means almost its opposite. It means "simple concept," as in *Fatal Attraction:* An innocent smile at a party turns a married man's life upside down and put his family in mortal jeopardy.

Sometimes a title is its own high concept, as with Margaret Mitchell's best-selling novel *Gone with the Wind,* the extended logline of which would be: "Against the backdrop of the great Civil War, a narcissistic Southern beauty obsessed with idyllic love struggles to reconstruct her life and finds that her true love is closer than she thinks."

High concept is a story that will compel the broadest audiences to watch the movie after hearing a pitch of only a few, or sometimes even one, word(s):

Psycho
Room
Anger Management
Sleepless in Seattle
Armageddon

Unwanted Attentions (title changed by NBC to *Stalker: Shadow of Obsession*)

Vertigo

Jaws

How to Lose a Guy in Ten Days

American Sniper

Unfaithful

Four Weddings and a Funeral

San Andreas

Black Hawk Down

Panic Room

Selma

Runaway Bride

Bridge of Spies

Don't Tell Mom the Babysitter's Dead

Home Alone

Cabin Fever

Die Hard

Ex Machina

These examples of high concept are pitched by their very titles. It's enough to hear the title—and know that Adam Sandler and Jack Nicholson star—to compel audiences to the box office to see *Anger Management*.

"*Die Hard* on a boat," was allegedly the logline that led to the sale of Steven Seagall's *Under Siege*.

Sicario: Recruited to assist in an undercover operation targeting a Mexican drug lord, a rooky FBI agent finds her moral standards put to the extreme test when she finds herself in the middle of a plan that goes far beyond the boundaries of law.

Creed: A young boxer who's the son of Rocky Balboa's onetime nemesis, Apollo Creed, travels to Philadelphia to plead for Rocky's help.

Titles like *The Fisher King, Seven Days in May, Snow Falling on Cedars, The Shipping News* may be evocative, but do *not* express a high concept that will instantly lure audiences. Though such titles may get lucky and become successful movies, in today's blockbuster market they'd be swimming upstream.

Nothing is more important to marketing your story than a "high concept logline" that makes it immediately stand out from all those stories that are subtle, nuanced, and difficult to pitch, and that depend entirely upon "execution." Here are some more examples that have led my companies or others to sales:

- "Jurassic Shark!" (the two-word description given our client Steve Alten's *Meg* by ICM-agent Jeff Robinov, who spearheaded a "preempt" from Disney for $1.1 million; the story was then re-sold to Newline, and then to Warner Brothers)

- When the most obnoxious guy in the world realizes he's become an asshole on a false premise, he makes a list of all the people he's wronged and sets out to repay them one by one. (John Scott Shepherd's *Henry's List of Wrongs,* sold to New Line Pictures for $1.6 million).

- *Life or Something Like It:* An ambitious and self-involved reporter is sparked into action to change the pattern of her life when she interviews a street-psychic who tells her that her life is meaningless—and that she's going to die—soon.

- *The Madam's Family:* The true "Canal Street Brothel" story of three generations of madams and their battle against persecution by the FBI.

- *The Lost Valentine:* A man and woman find the love of their lifetimes when they're brought together to memorialize the bittersweet story of a doomed World War II pilot and the wife who promised to wait forever for his return.

- *The Kill Martin Club:* Advertising mogul Martin Pickford gets murdered—a lot!

- *Three Men Seeking Monsters:* Three over-grown teenage cryptozoologists go on a cross-country trek to investigate monster sightings—only to discover the legends they're exploiting are real.

The "logline" is a one-line description of the story, very much like the one-liners you would read when you click GUIDE on your remote. ("Hollywood makes movies you can advertise on TV," says pro Joe Roth). *Jaws* can be advertised, visually or verbally, as "Shark bad. Kill shark!" After all, television is where you hope your work will end up eventually, so making buyers think it can fit there is the smartest first step to selling.

It's not necessary for your logline to mention character names. A strong character trait will do—with a dramatic teaser about the story. All loglines go back to the ancient storyteller's formula: "What would happen if a character like x ended up in a situation like y?" You can add a specific catchword that quickly tells the reader what the story is about. Is it about love, greed, obsession murder, family turmoil? Once you're set on one or two words you can continue from there, adding a few more economical adjectives and verbs to make up your logline.

Consider these further examples, grouped by "genre":

A woman or a family in jeopardy:

The Shallows: While riding the waves at a remote beach, a young surfer finds herself injured and stranded just twenty miles from shore on a buoy—as a great white shark begins stalking her.

Cape Fear: A lawyer's family is stalked by a man he once helped put in prison.

Room: After being abducted, abused, and imprisoned for seven years in a small windowless room, a mother devises a bold escape plan.

An ordinary woman in extraordinary circumstances:

The Danish Girl: What happens if the husband you adore needs to be a woman?

Woman in Gold: Six decades after World War II, a Jewish octogenarian begins a quest to reclaim the artwork confiscated from her family by the Nazis and now proudly celebrated by the Austrian government—including a famed Gustav Klimt masterpiece.

Men on a mission:

Saving Private Ryan: US soldiers try to save their comrade who's stationed behind enemy lines.

Bridge of Spies: At the height of the Cold War in 1960, the downing of an American spy plane and the pilot's subsequent capture by the Soviets draws Brooklyn attorney James Donovan into the middle of an intense effort to secure the aviator's release.

American Pie: Four teenage boys make a pact to lose their virginity by prom night.

Man against nature:

The Martian: He was left behind—on Mars.

The Revenant: A frontiersman fights for survival after being mauled by a grizzly and left for dead by his own hunting team.

Man or woman against the system:

Spotlight: A Boston news team sets out to expose numerous cases of child molestation and cover up on the part of the local Catholic Archdiocese.

Concussion: A pathologist uncovers the truth about brain damage in football players who suffer repeated concussions and comes up against the corporate power of the NFL.

People vs. Larry Flynt: A pornography publisher becomes the unlikely defender of free speech.

Class Action: A female attorney finds that opposing counsel is her own father, and must choose between her corporate client and justice.

A woman escaping from something or someone she loves:

The Perfect Guy: After breaking up with her boyfriend, a professional woman gets involved with a man who seems almost too good to be true.

Enough: On the run from an abusive husband, a young mother begins to train herself to fight back.

Far from the Madding Crowd: Elevated to landowner via inheritance, a beautiful and headstrong young woman, afraid of losing her independence, runs from the attentions of three very different suitors.

Sleeping with the Enemy: A young woman fakes her own death in an attempt to escape her nightmarish marriage, but discovers it's impossible to elude her controlling husband.

Here are the dramatic elements filmmakers long to spot in our onslaught of daily email queries: A high concept logline that makes a story out of universal—

- human emotions: fear, love, hate, envy, etc.

- deadly sins: anger, greed, lust, etc.

- plot motivators: betrayal, vengeance, discovery, rebirth, survival, etc.

- virtues: loyalty, faith, responsibility, etc.

—and incarnates those elements in characters we can care about, relate to, and root for to shape an "original story" that feels both fresh and relevant to today's global market.

If you can do that, and your writing effectively expresses your vision, you're only steps away from financial success and recognition on the biggest screen of all.

6 | Market Your Story

ONCE YOU'VE GOTTEN a great treatment ready, use it to create a full "marketing array" consisting of the treatment, your logline, and a half-page pitch.

A "logline," or one-line pitch:

Films are marketed to audiences with "one liners" known as "loglines" or "pitches"—a one- or two-sentence "pitch line," aka "elevator pitch," the kind you'd use to get someone to want to see more if you had their attention for fifteen seconds: "He invented a machine to bring pleasure, and turned the Victorian world upside down" (*Hysteria*). Some of the best one-liners end up as titles: *Liar, Liar, Bruce Almighty, Friends with Benefits*. If your novel has a great logline, it's already a candidate for film: "She never expected love to appear at her doorstep," is a one-line pitch of *The Bridges of Madison County*.

One-page pitch aka "the one-pager":

Start with your logline, then tell your story in one or two compelling paragraphs, highlighting the protagonist and antagonist, three acts clearly defined to present the arc of the story as well as other defining characteristics such as a love interest, humor, irony, and overriding theme.

Next, to protect your story and document your claim to having written it, register your marketing array at http://www.wgawregistry.org/. You don't have to be a member to register. When your story material is received, it's sealed in an envelope and the date and time are recorded. A numbered certificate is returned to you which serves as the official documentation of registration.

WGAW **WRITERS GUILD OF AMERICA,** WEST

Make an inventory of anyone and everyone you know connected with television or film, and get their email addresses. Think of this step as chumming the waters, by throwing out bait to attract the big fish. Send them the logline only, asking if they'd be interested in *advising* you on how to get this story to the screen. If they're interested, they'll ask if you have more. That's when you can send them your one-pager.

If they're interested in your one-pager, they'll ask if you have more. That's when you should send them your treatment, which will state your WGAW registration discreetly at the bottom margin of page one.

If they're interested in your treatment, they'll ask if you have more. Then and only then tell them you have a manuscript or a published novel, but that they're different from the treatment which was written to turn your novel into a film. Or, if you have a script, now's the time to let them know that.

The good thing about having a script ready is that it can save a year or more of development, along with tens of thousands of dollars of development funds. The bad thing is that if your script isn't superb, it may kill all interest in the story. A bad script is worse than no script. No one wants to start with a bad script because WGA rules are such that it must be both "credited" and "compensated"—and suddenly the whole thing approaches the "life is too short" list.

If you don't have a single contact in Hollywood, direct or indirect, how do you find someone who can help you? You'll discover that, if you try to send your treatment or query by snail mail to a major motion picture studio without an industry introduction, you'll receive your treatment back in an official-looking brown envelope stating on the outside that it is being "returned unread," and that you might consider submitting it through an agent or attorney.

This rude response has an understandable history. Studios are often regarded as having "deep pockets." For that reason, in our extremely litigious society, they are often targets for nuisance lawsuits from authors claiming that their story or idea was stolen. Receiving a story, therefore, is fraught with danger for the studios or major producers. They much prefer receiving a story from someone inside the industry with whom they're already acquainted and can trust *not* to be litigious at the drop of a hat.

How do you meet an insider if you're on the outside? Check out screenwriting contests that can give you industry exposure like the Nicholl Fellowship Competition, Final Draft's The Big Break Contest, Slamdance Screenplay Competition, or American Zoetrope Screenplay Contest. There's no shortage of writers conferences and festivals you can attend like the Austin Film Festival Pitch Competition, Santa Fe Screenwriting Conference, Hollywood Pitch Festival, The Great American Pitchfest, Thrillerfest-Pitchfest, Scriptapalooza or Story Expo—where industry folk—including agents, literary managers, attorneys, and studio execs—appear to share their insight into the changing industry. Check the conference brochure for the list of attendees and do your research. When you identify an insider who might relate to your story, attend the conferences and find a way to meet him or her in person.

New to the party are virtual pitch fests like EHollywoodLive—an Internet version of Fade In's Hollywood Pitch Fest.

You're looking for contacts that produce films LIKE your story, getting to know better the industry you want to be part of. IMDb (Internet Movie Database) is a great resource for checking filmmakers' credits and for gathering some contact information.

Yes, this will take some research on your part, as you get to know better the industry you want to be part of.

If you find an agent, manager, or attorney—celebrate. Then approach them by email.

If you have no luck finding a representative, you can also try to find a screenwriter to write your script. Choose an expert with produced credits or at least several sales. Read two or more of his or her sample scripts to make sure you agree with his or her sensitivities. Make a deal to pay the screenwriter as little as he or she will take upfront, with the standard WGA minimum compensation to come from the budget of the film. If you make a deal with a good screenwriter, celebrate. Beware bringing on an inexperienced screenwriter who's willing to "spec" your script. Remember, a bad script is worse than no script at all.

Of course you might consider writing the script yourself. Screenplays cost money and time, which inhibits the acquisition of your novel by notoriously frugal indie filmmakers. But screenplays are ten times harder to write than novels. There's *no* room for "forgiveness" in a script. If your character happens to be wearing a red cap in the opening scene, the audience will keep wondering about that cap until it "pays off." If it doesn't pay off they'll fret about it over drinks after the show. Repeat warning: A bad screenplay is *worse* than no screenplay at all. The chances that you, as the novelist, can be objective enough to write your own screenplay are small—but not entirely impossible. William Faulkner wrote the script for *The Sound and the Fury,* and did an outstanding job. Other examples include Michael Crichton's *Jurassic Park* and Truman Capote's *Breakfast at Tiffany's.*

Buy and learn Final Draft, the standard Hollywood scriptwriting program.

Final Draft

Before you begin your script, read *at least twenty screenplays* of films you love. Two great places to find screenplays to download free are IMSDb—Internet Movie Screenplay Database (http://www.imsdb.com/) and Drew's Script-o-Rama (http://www.script-o-rama.com/).

As you read, notice everything about them. Read as though you were writing them. It might even help to type out your favorite one in your new Final Draft program, to get the hang of what a good script feels like.

Also read at least two good books on screenwriting, like Syd Field's *Screenplay,* Todd Klick's *Beat by Beat,* Blake Snyder's *Save the Cat!,* David Trottier's *The Screenwriter's Bible,* Linda Seger's *Making a Good Script Great,* or Pen Densham's *Riding the Alligator: Strategies for a Career in Screenplay Writing… and Not Getting Eaten.*

When you feel ready, jot down a first draft without stopping to revise. I've known writers who can write a screenplay in three or four days. Their managers tell them *never* to admit that to the buyers, but it's true.

Then register your draft with the WGA.

Set it aside for three weeks or more after you've asked ten of your worst critics to read it and tear it apart. Rewrite it, taking their criticism when you see its merits, ignoring it when you don't. Have another five people—not family, not close friends—read it and do the same.

If everyone thinks your script is great, celebrate!

Now go through the marketing process again, this time with the script as your ultimate offering. Don't be surprised if most of the studios, independent production companies, agencies, and management companies say they "do not accept unsolicited submissions." You're up against the "rule of 10,000." That is the estimated number of SCRIPTS that get offered to Hollywood each year. Maybe ten to twenty of them find a production home, but don't despair: 90% or more of these orphan scripts are hopelessly unprofessional. That's where you hold the edge, because *yours* is not.

Hint: Entertainment attorneys are often the easiest route for the complete outsider to find representation, for the simple reason that you can *retain* them—meaning that you're paying for their time.

You could also find one who will do it for a percentage of what you make (3-5% is normal).

When you succeed in finding representation, your rep will probably give you feedback on the script. Get used to that. It will keep happening until the day your film goes before the cameras—and throughout production as well. It's always about sharpening the flame, and the professional response to another set of changes is, "I'm willing to do whatever it takes to make this story as powerful as it can be." If you're lucky enough to get a star involved, expect to be asked to make more changes to suit him or her. After all, the producer, director, and stars are where they are because they've already been down the road you want to travel many times. You're fortunate to get their feedback, and to get them invested in your story. Fix the script accordingly. If you don't agree with their changes, explain why. Maybe you've already tried what they're suggesting and can tell them why it won't work, or why it weakens the story. This exchange, known as "creative dialogue," shouldn't be taken personally—by either side. It's all about making the film better.

When your rep is satisfied that the script is as good as it can be, he or she will begin approaching allies in the industry to get the script set up. That's called "taking it out to the town."

Don't ask him or her for a detailed strategy in advance. I always say that setting up a movie is like three-dimensional chess. You can waste time strategizing your first ten moves, but every move changes all the players on the board, so best to take a single move, then regroup and see where you stand.

FAQ:

These are all excellent questions that you should explore as soon as you've brought an entertainment attorney into your life; but you should also explore them when you sign with a representative. You can't go wrong by asking questions, especially if you ask them in a friendly way. And it's even better if you ask them before they become an issue of concern to you:

Q. How long should one wait without hearing anything before asking?

A. There's no right or wrong answer to this. It will depend on the exact situation. You might start a practice of "checking in" every three or four weeks, unless the person you're checking in on asks you to do it more or less frequently.

Q. How long is the "average" wait?

A. Again, there's no right or wrong answer. Some deals close in ninety days, but one I closed took three years because the merchandising involved with the film was so complicated—and the studio management entirely changed three times!

Q. When something major happens, should you expect to be included?

A. I hate being repetitious, but that too depends on the exact situation. Certainly your attorney should inform you if something major happens.

Q. What is the etiquette of it all? Is it okay to be in direct touch with your prospective buyer, or do you have to let your attorney handle everything?

A. The general protocol of Hollywood dealings is that you, the "artist," deal *only* with artistic matters with your buyer—leaving all business matters to your representative and attorney who normally work in tandem during the closing of a deal. It's dangerous to break that protocol because the exec on the other side is used to it and doesn't want to risk anything negative clouding the positive creative relationship he or she needs to have with you.

Q. What issues are okay to take into your own hands?

A. It is *your* story and *your* career. You can always do that, but weigh the possibilities before you do. What are the chances of your improving the situation? What are the chances of you making it worse?

7 | Making the Deal

THE FIRST RULE is: if you're offered a deal, *make* it.

It's fine to negotiate a deal you're offered for your story. But all too many deals each year are negotiated to death. Ask your representative to explain the parameters of the deal you've been offered. What is possible? What is standard? What are the WGA's guidelines and minimum? Don't demand the moon, especially if this is your first

On location in New York for *Life or Something Like It.*

deal. Deals fall apart all the time because the desperate writer's greed is activated by the very whiff of a Hollywood deal. As in any walk of life, *your first deal is unlikely to be your best deal.* But it is that all-important foot in the door that matters most, so don't let it slip away.

Don't be surprised at how long your deal takes to close. Studio legal departments are normally overworked and underwater, a handful of attorneys handling every contract the studio's involved in. You have to keep lighting fires under them to get their attention back to your deal. That, I'm afraid, is normal; you don't have to like it, but don't take it personally. Write something else while you're waiting.

Here's what you can expect financially from a writer's deal, which are almost always structured as "option-purchase agreements":

1. An "option price," ranging from $1 to $100,000 or more depending on the perceived value of the "underlying material," with the emphasis being on the low end depending on *your* and *your story's* visibility. The option will be paid upon execution of the agreement, which can take months of legal back and forth from the time the buyer says yes. The "option period" is normally eighteen months, but it is nearly always renewable for a second eighteen months and sometimes for an additional period. During the option period the buyer has the right to develop the story, doing all that's necessary to prepare it to be filmed.

2. A "purchase price," averaging 1% to 2.5% of the budget of the film (according to WGA guidelines), normally paid on the first day of principal photography. The option price is normally subtracted from the purchase price,

and together they are called "fixed compensation."

3. A "participation" in the "back end," also known as "contingent compensation," meaning your share of any profits that trickle down to the producer ("producer's share"). So rare is it to actually receive that participation from a major studio that some cynics in the business refer to participation as "monkey points." I leave you to imagine why.

4. Your name in the front end credits and paid advertising of the film, depending on what you contribute, for example: "Based on the novel by You," or "Inspired by the book by You." This credit is governed strictly by the WGA, which alone has the right to grant a writing credit on a film or television show. A producer who promises you a "credit no matter what" is to be suspected, since no one but the WGA has the right to promise such credit.

The WGA has a procedure for screen credits called NOTICES OF TENTATIVE WRITING CREDIT. For the production company, the filing of the NTWC with the Guild sets in motion the Guild mechanism for determination of credits so that the credits can be finalized in a timely fashion. From the writer's perspective, the NTWC advises of the proposed credit and the deadline to register a protest, if necessary, of such credit. For the Guild, the NTWC offers an opportunity to ensure that the proposed writing credit and any and all source material credit comply with the mandates of the "MBA" (Theatrical and Television Basic Agreement) and Guild policy.

Writers may only be credited in the manner set forth in the MBA unless a waiver is granted. Allowable writing credits include "Written by," "Screenplay by," "Story by," "Screen Story by," "Adaptation by," "Narration Written by," and "Based on Characters Created by." In certain circumstances, the writing credit can be combined with the credit to the Director and/or the Producer.

Appendix B gives a generic boilerplate example of an option-purchase agreement.

When your deal finally closes, celebrate. It's a rare occurrence, and ought to be recognized for the achievement it is. There are plenty of bumps along the road to come that will discourage you, but right now stop and take a rest, celebrate, and pat yourself on the back.

How much influence on your story's film development can you expect to have?

Even If you were paid a substantial option amount, you can expect, honestly, very little—no matter what you're told in the beginning. Your attorney should ask for meaningful consultation, and to be invited to the set; but that doesn't always happen, especially if you express your displeasure to the wrong person. The producers have the right to remove you from the set if you cause any problems to the flow of the production. They now own

68

your story, and are protective of their right to control what happens to it. That's what they paid for, after all.

You need to develop the idea that you've created this powerful flame with your story, and that you've now handed over your flame to someone who, hopefully, will enhance it, clarify it, and make it burn even brighter. Trust your instincts on this. When someone is interested in your story, find out as much as you can about him or her (use www.imdb.com for this, to begin with). If you don't like the films they've made why would you give them your precious story? Getting a bad film made is not particularly helpful to your future career, no matter how much money it brought you.

The perils of "development hell."

During the option period, you may well find yourself in what Hollywood calls "development hell." I've worked on one film that was in that hell for thirteen years at one studio, only to be yanked from that studio when a final renewal came up because my client, right or wrong, was convinced there was no real intention to produce the film—despite the hundreds of thousands the studio spent on it. Now it's at another studio, starting off on a whole new road to the screen. *Meg,* which appears in 2018 from Warner Brothers, was sold first to Disney where it languished for three years of personnel turmoil at the studio and then fizzled during the regime change that followed. Then we re-sold it to New Line, where after several years it came very close to being made—with a major director attached, locations chosen, models constructed, etc. Suddenly the studio got cold feet about the director's ability to bring the film in on a budget low enough for them to handle—and it was abandoned. Finally it was re-sold to Warner Brothers, who by that time had purchased New Line, who moved ahead with the film. This town is filled with stories of well-known and well-paid screenwriters who've *never* had a "greenlight," despite the excellence of their scripts. The odds are not in your favor. But please adopt my slogan: "The odds don't apply to me." Optimism and determination are the only sane approach to "herding cats" (another metaphor for getting a movie made).

Do I need an attorney?

Yes, you do, but an entertainment attorney, not any other kind. And as soon as you find a reliable one keep him or her forever. A trusted attorney is invaluable, especially because you're going to need a professional to hold your hand as you go through the Hollywood learning curve.

As frustrating as their apparent lethargy can be to the impatient writer, attorneys are the glue that holds the industry together. They have relationships—with agents, executives, financers, and other attorneys—and their relationships become yours.

You can easily find an entertainment attorney by referral from any attorney you trust—or on

Google. I heartily suggest finding a lawyer who knows Hollywood in either Los Angeles or New York, or both. When? As early in your career as you feel comfortable doing it, the earlier the better but certainly no later than the day you receive an actual deal for one of your stories.

8 | Do It Yourself

IF THE PROCESS we've just outlined doesn't please you, how else can you get your book made into a film?

Money makes things happen. If you have access to funding, take the time-honored entrepreneurial route of making the film yourself. Aside from the thrill of it, this approach

- Keeps you more proactive, involved in all phases of your film's development and production;

- Keeps you in control. You will *not* be in control if you sell your rights to someone else;

- Maximizes your financial profit from your film. You'll be paid as the creator and owner of the underlying rights, for the screenplay (if you write it), and for your role as a producer.

There are at least two paths to making the film yourself.

Shoot the film yourself.

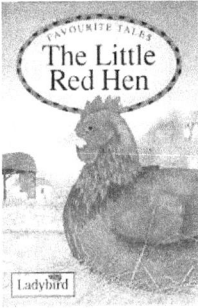

"The Little Red Hen" was my favorite fairytale growing up, about the farmyard chicken that wanted to bake some bread and asked all the animals for help; when they all looked the other way, she baked it all by herself—and kept it for her and her chicks. The little red hen is what you become if you do it yourself. You're chief cook and bottle washer, and determined to get it done no matter what the other barnyard animals say or do. And you're in complete control.

This is the heroic path taken by enterprising and aspiring directors like Robert Rodriguez, who made his student film *El Mariachi* for around $7,500. He was courted by several studios, and ended up with a two-year deal with Columbia Pictures—and the following year won the coveted Audience Award at Sundance. Rodriguez hired the actors for half-days so he wouldn't have to buy them lunch and, since he couldn't afford an audio crew, shot them with their lips away from camera so dialogue could be dubbed in "postproduction."

Eduardo Sanchez and Daniel Myrick, Florida college students looking for a break, broke through with their *Blair Witch Project*, which rumor says cost them less than $60,000 (and made $249 million worldwide!). Oren Peli made *Paranormal Activity* for $15,000.

73

It's often possible to talk local postproduction studios into lending their editing bays for next to nothing, and not unusual that they and others are happy to contribute "film stock," food, locations, and even cameras just for the fun of making a movie. Obviously the DIY filmmaker can't be shy about asking for assistance.

Once you've got the film finished, you'll go through the same process outlined above with agents, literary managers, sales agents, film distributors, and attorneys. Only this time you're asking them to look at an actual film, not just words in search of a film. That substantially ups your chances of getting attention. Just make sure that at least one of your actors has a recognizable track record of notable films.

All this is assuming your film is good, but that goes without saying, right?

If you're a first-timer, each one of these hurdles will be a challenge. You're operating in the most creative of industries—so don't hesitate to use your creativity to the max, thinking outside the box, to accomplish what needs to be accomplished.

Instead of sending out pitch emails, now you'll be sending trailers instead—and posting them on YouTube, where filmmakers are "discovered" by Hollywood every week. As your number of views increase, so do your chances of catching the attention of someone in a position to get your story to the world.

Find a co-producer.

If you aren't willing to risk your story's future on your own filmmaking abilities, you can also find a producer who's excited enough about your story to work with you through the development and production process.

If you manage to partner with a pro who's been there and done that, you're in a perfect position to learn every phase of the filmmaking process outlined in chapter one.

9 | In Production

THOSE ARE THE magic words you want to hear, and they are music to my ears even after decades of making films happen. It's almost a miracle when that day comes that the cameras begin to roll in Seattle, Vancouver, Minneapolis, Montreal, London, New Orleans, Dallas, New York, Los Angeles, Atlanta—just some of the cities I've had the pleasure of shooting in.

On set with *The Madams Family* in New Orleans.

Definitely time for another celebration.

But then what?

Hopefully, you're invited to the set. If you're invited, by all means go!

Be respectful, and observe professionals in action turning your dream into a cinematic reality. Stay out of their way. Better to be reserved, and let them draw you out. Film crews are usually dead serious, focused on the work at hand; however, they're also naturally curious, naturally friendly and they *will* draw you out if they see you respecting their work and staying out of their way. Be brief and direct in your answers. Then it becomes fun, and you'll discover they—and the director— may start asking you questions about what they're about to film. Observe. This is a major learning curve for you, and if you get to hang around a set as the brilliant writers Stephen and Jonah Lisa Dyer did for most of the shoot of *Hysteria,* you'll learn things that will make you a better writer. Be a fly on the wall. It all sounds tremendously exciting to first-timers, but it is plain hard and often tedious work.

Don't act *entitled;* be humble. You are privileged to be there, where "a village" has taken on the task of *building* your movie. Make it a rule never to cause delays in the process. I'll never forget the time, on the set of *Life or Something Like It,* when I found Angelina hopping up and down on one leg while waiting for the next setup to complete. "Are you okay?" I asked. "Yeah. I just have to pee real bad."

"Well, geez," I answered. "Go pee. It'll be fine."

"I just *hate* to cause any kind of holdup," she said, giving me a grateful smile as she ran to her trailer. That is what real professionals are like.

Don't volunteer to move the lights or the camera. These are all professionals with expensive equipment. They know what they're doing. Just watch them and learn. Show up on time and you'll win their hearts. Stay till the last man leaves and they'll adore you.

When you leave the set for the first time, don't forget to celebrate. You deserve to savor this moment.

Your Premier

Your deal will have included invitations to the film's premier. Dress nicely, and go there, with your favorite person, no matter how far away it is. It could be a once-in-a-lifetime occasion.

Observe the audience. See how they react. Even though they're "friends of the film," their reactions give you a sense of how the film is working. I bumped into Adrian Lyne one night in the lobby after a random screening of *Jacob's Ladder*. He was sneaking out the door, and later told me he always liked to go anonymously to see for himself how audiences are reacting.

Hang around in the lobby afterwards to say hello to the cast and crew and thank them. Don't expect praise, but be happily surprised when you receive it. Do the same thing when your film comes to your local theater. That's where the audience reaction will give you true insight into how well the film succeeded.

The next day, go back to work on your next script. You'll save yourself endless anxiety in this business if you keep busy on your next project while waiting for something to happen with your present project. See Appendix A for "Life in the Waiting Room."

For commercial independent movies we're always looking for high-energy *action; sci-fi;* life-changing *drama; romantic comedy;* bestselling *fantasy;* and *family animation* (probably the most lucrative of all film genres).

Remember that none of these guidelines—descriptive observations of what gets picked up for filmmaking rather than prescriptive rules—guarantees your success. But they stack the cards in your favor. The more *proactive* you become in the world of filmmaking, the sooner you will succeed! These aren't God-given rules. There was no set of commandments that somebody lugged down from a mountain to the rest of us. They're just common sense principles of storytelling that go back as far as *The Iliad* and *Odyssey* and the Bible and Upanishads.

You can break rules, be experimental, as long as you're successful. One of my favorite novels-into-film, William Wharton's *Birdy* plays havoc with the novel's order—and brilliantly succeeds because even with its jumping around in time it jumps at such dramatic moments that the audience is swept along with it. *Memento*, from a short story by Jonathan Nolan, has a most unconventional structure because the end and the beginning are interchangeable; but so powerful is the drama that you forget about the beginning until you get it again in the third act—and it takes you by surprise.

Whether storytelling is by Alfred Hitchcock or Walt Disney or J.J. Abrams, they all follow the same principles—not rules. I want to emphasize that because writers naturally react to the word rules with, "I'm an artist. I don't follow rules." So these are not rules. These are observations about what makes successful commercial storytelling in Hollywood movies. Instead of rules that somebody makes up and creates a world from, these are just guidelines:

The world has already been created; now let's look at what the world consists of and see if we can distill that into "things to do" and "things to avoid" that we can pass on to everybody out there who's disappointed their novel hasn't been sold as a film—yet.

GO FOR IT! NEVER GIVE UP.

BOOKS INTO FILMS

Action:

- James Bond series from the novels by Ian Fleming

- *The Bourne Identity* (series) from the novels by Robert Ludlum

- *The Girl with the Dragon Tattoo* (trilogy) from the novels by Stieg Larsson

- *Jurassic Park* (series) from the novel by Michael Crichton

- *The Lord of the Rings* (trilogy) by J.R.R. Tolkien

- *The Hobbit* (trilogy) from the novel by J.R.R. Tolkien

- *The Last of the Mohicans* from the novel by James Fennimore Cooper

- *Tinker, Tailor, Soldier, Spy* from the novel by John le Carré

Drama:

- *Birdy* from the novel by William Wharton

- *Rosemary's Baby* from the novel by Ira Levin

- *One Flew over the Cuckoo's Nest* from the novel by Ken Kesey

- *The Prince of Tides* from the novel by Pat Conroy

- *The Grapes of Wrath* from the novel by John Steinbeck

- *The Wolf of Wall Street* from the memoir by Jordan Belfort

- *Gone Girl* from the novel by Gillian Flynn

- *The Hunt for Red October* from the novel by Tom Clancy

- *The Third Man* from the novel by Graham Greene

- *Water for Elephants* from the novel by Sara Gruen

- *The Color Purple* from the novel by Alice Walker

- *Life of Pi* from the novel by Yann Martel

Romance:

- *The Notebook* from the novel by Nicholas Sparks

- *The Bridges of Madison County* from the novel by Robert James Waller

- *The Devil Wears Prada* from the novel by Lauren Weisberger

- *Gone with the Wind* from the novel by Margaret Mitchell

- *Love Story* from the novel by Erich Segal

- *Pride and Prejudice* from the novel by Jane Austen

- *The Ghost and Mrs. Muir* from the novel by Josephine Leslie

- *Portrait of Jenny* from the novel by Robert Nathan

- *Practical Magic* from the novel by Alice Hoffman

- *The World of Suzie Wong* from the novel by Richard Mason

Young Adult:

- *Twilight* (trilogy) from the novels by Stephenie Meyer

- *Harry Potter* (series) from the novels by J. K. Rowling

- *The Hunger Games* (trilogy) from the novels by Suzanne Collins

- *Divergent* (trilogy) from the novels by Veronica Roth

- *The Maze Runner* from the novel by James Dashner

- *The Fault in Our Stars* from the novel by John Green

- *The Perks of Being a Wallflower* from the novel by Stephen Chbosky

Animation:

- *The Jungle Book* from the novel by Rudyard Kipling

- *Alice in Wonderland* from the novel by Lewis Carroll

- *Fantastic Mr. Fox* from the novel by Roald Dahl

- *How to Train Your Dragon* loosely based on the British book series by Cressida Cowell

- *Shrek* loosely based on William Steig's fairy tale picture book

- *Where the Wild Things Are* from the picture book by Maurice Sendak

- *Winnie the Pooh and the Honey Tree* from the novel by A.A. Milne

- *Peter Pan* from the novel by James M. Barrie

- *One Hundred and One Dalmatians* from the novel by Dodie Smith

True Stories:

- *Spotlight* from stories by the Spotlight team of *The Boston Globe*

- *The Big Short,* based on the nonfiction book *The Big Short: Inside the Doomsday Machine,* by Michael Lewis

- *Charlie Wilson's War,* from *Charlie Wilson's War: The Extraordinary Story of How the Wildest Man in Congress and a Rogue CIA Agent*

Changed the History of Our Times by George Crile

- *Black Hawk Down,* from the book by the same title by Mark Bowden

- *Mean Girls,* from *Queen Bees and Wannabees* by Rosalind Wisemanby

- *American Sniper,* based on the memoir of Chris Kyle

- *Adaptation,* based on *The Orchid Thief* by Susan Orlean

- *Theory of Everything,* from Jane Hawking's *Traveling to Infinity*

- *Seabiscuit,* from Laura Hillenbrand's *Seabiscuit: An American Legend*

- *The Pianist* adapted from the autobiography *The Pianist: The Extraordinary True Story of One Man's Survival in Warsaw, 1935–1945* by Wladyslaw Szpilman

- *All the President's Men,* from the book by Carl Bernstein and Bob Woodward

- *The Kennedy Detail* from the book by Jerry Blaine and Lisa McCubbin

Life in the Waiting Room

How Long Do I Have to Wait?

Writers ask me that all the time, becoming impatient and anxious that their story is taking so long to become a book or a movie. My answer surprises them:

Don't wait at all.

Waiting is a massive waste of time, and can lead to depression, existential despair, and who knows what else. *Do something* while you wait. Plant another seed, cultivate it, train it to grow straight. And while it's taking its sweet time to bud and then bloom, do something else. Start a book!

Back in the sixties, I reviewed a great book by Barry Stevens: *Don't Push the River, It Flows by Itself.* Every project has its own clock and will come to fruition when that clock reaches the appointed hour. Other than keeping that project on track the best you can, there's nothing you can do—other than financing it yourself (a serious option, by the way), to speed up that clock. By the nature of things, that clock is secret, which means extra frustration for the creator—unless you refuse to wait.

Recently my dear producing partner Norman Stephens and I produced a sweet little Christmas movie, *Angels in the Snow.* I had only been trying to get that movie produced for twenty years! Sold it to TNN once, came close to a deal at Hallmark another time. What was I doing for twenty years? Producing nearly thirty other films, managing hundreds of books, writing and publishing books of my own, playing tennis, traveling, having a wonderful life. Not waiting.

Waiting makes people neurotic. If I allowed myself to express my neurosis, as many writers have not yet learned not to do, I would drive those involved in making my story into a book or film crazy—and risk losing their support. The question I hate hearing the most— "What's going on?" — is one I stop myself from asking. My job, when I'm in charge of moving a story forward, is to "get the ball out of my court" as efficiently and as soon as possible. Then, on that project, I have to wait for it to be returned to my court. Very few actual events occur along the way, leaving a huge gap of dead time in between them, like super novae separated by light years of space.

It's not dead time if you use it for something else creative.

If the glacial pace of the creative business fills you with dread, you're in the wrong business or you're dealing with it the wrong way.

Don't wait. Do. As the inimitable Ray Bradbury put it: *"Start writing more. It'll get rid of all those moods you're having."*

Generic Option-Purchase Agreement

As of August

_____

_____

_____

Dear Messrs. _____ and _____:

This will confirm the agreement between _____ ("Purchaser") and both of you (collectively "you") with respect to the original, unpublished, unexploited screenplay entitled "_____" written by you (which, together with the title, themes, contents and characters, and all translations, adaptations, and other versions thereof now or hereafter owned by you, whether now existing or hereafter created, is hereinafter called the "Property").

In consideration of the parties' mutual promises, it is hereby agreed as follows:

1. OPTION

(a) You hereby exclusively and irrevocably grant to Purchaser two (2) consecutive options (the "Option"), each lasting for one (1) year, to purchase all rights in the Property as set forth in Paragraph 6 hereof (the "Rights"). The initial option period shall commence on the date on which you deliver this Agreement and all attachments hereto to Purchaser fully-executed. The initial option period may be extended by Purchaser for the second option period at any time prior to the expiration of the initial option period.

(b) The initial option period shall be at a cost of Two Thousand Five Hundred Dollars ($2,500), payable upon the full execution hereof. The second option period shall be at a cost of Two Thousand Dollars ($2,000), payable, if at all, not later than the expiration of the initial option period. The option payment with respect to the initial option period shall be applicable against the Purchase Price (as defined below). The option payment with respect to the second option period shall not apply against said Purchase Price.

(c) During the option period (and extensions thereof, if any), Purchaser shall have the right to engage in or arrange for preproduction with respect to motion pictures and/or other productions intended to be based on the Property. The first such motion picture or other production is referred to herein as the "Picture." If in connection with such preproduction another party is engaged by Purchaser to write screenplays or other materials based on the Property, all such writings shall be and remain Purchaser's sole and exclusive property (whether or not Purchaser exercises the Option hereunder).

2. PURCHASE PRICE. If Purchaser exercises the Option, the purchase price for the Rights shall be the following amount ("Purchase Price"), as applicable:

(a) Self-Financing or Co-Financing. If Purchaser self-finances or co-finances the Picture with a third party, Twenty Thousand Dollars ($20,000), less the initial option payment. In the event Purchaser co-finances the Picture with a third party (as opposed to an outright sale or self-financing), then, depending upon the amount of the budget of the Picture, Purchaser agrees to use reasonable efforts to increase the Purchase Price. In the event Purchaser enters into a binding unconditional agreement with a third party pursuant to which such third party acquires outright all rights in and to the Property, then you shall be entitled to receive the greater of said Twenty Thousand Dollars ($20,000) or one-third (1/3) of the net profits generated from such sale. For purposes of this Paragraph 2(a) only, "net profits" shall be determined as follows: all gross amounts actually received by Purchaser from the sale of all rights in the Property, less the following deductions: (i) Purchaser's actual out-of-pocket costs incurred in connection with developing and producing the Picture; plus (ii) an overhead charge in an amount equal to fifteen percent (15%) of (i) plus interest on (i), and (ii) at the prime rate charged by the Bank of America (Los Angeles Branch) at the time, plus two percent (2%).

(b) Third Party Financing. If a studio or other third party fully finances the Picture, in lieu of the amount set forth in (a), an amount equal to two and one-half percent (2-1/2%) of the final approved budget of the Picture, less the initial option payment, up to a maximum ceiling of Two Hundred and Fifty Thousand Dollars ($250,000). The "final approved budget" shall be the going-in budget of the Picture, exclusive of interest, financing charges, completion bond fees, overhead and any contingency.

(c) Exercise Date. The Option, if exercised, shall be exercised by written notice or by commencement of principal photography of the Picture, whichever is sooner.

3. NET PROFITS

If the Option is exercised and the Picture is produced and released based on the Rights granted and material written by you hereunder, and if pursuant to a final credit determination under this Agreement you shall receive screenplay credit in connection with the Picture, provided that Purchaser does not sell outright the rights to produce the Picture to a third party, Purchaser will pay you:

(a) If you receive sole "screenplay by" or sole "written by" credit ("Sole Credit"), an amount equal to five percent (5%) of one hundred percent (100%) of the Net Profits of the Picture; and

(b) If you receive shared "screenplay by" or shared "written by" credit with any other writer or writers

("Shared Credit"), an amount equal to two and one-half percent (2-1/2%) of one hundred percent (100%) of the Net Profits of the Picture.

(c) In the event Purchaser solely finances the Picture, Purchaser shall have the right to, in lieu of the amounts set forth in subparagraph (a) or (b) above, elect to pay you either (i) five percent (5%) of Purchaser's Net Profits or (ii) five percent (5%) of the first $100,000 of Net Profits received by Purchaser, plus seven and one-half percent (7.5%) of the second $100,000 of Net Profits received by Purchaser, plus ten percent (10%) of the next Three Hundred Thousand Dollars ($300,000) of Net Profits received by Purchaser, and fifteen percent (15%) of the Net Profits received by Purchaser in excess of Five Hundred Thousand Dollars ($500,000). Purchaser's election under this paragraph shall be made prior to the date of commencement of principal photography.

The "Net Profits" referred to in this Agreement shall be computed, determined and payable in accordance with and subject to the definition of net profits applicable to Purchaser in its agreement with the distributor of the Picture, if there is one worldwide distributor of the Picture which provides the entire financing for the Picture, and if there is more than one distributor and/or the single worldwide distributor does not provide the entire financing for the Picture, then in accordance with Purchaser's standard definition of net profits, which shall in any event provide for, without limitation, recoupment of all of Purchaser's costs in connection with the Picture, interest and overhead of 15%. Included in the cost of production shall be a producer's fee to Purchaser in an amount not to exceed Two Hundred Thousand Dollars ($200,000). The definition of Net Profits accorded to you pursuant to this Paragraph 3 shall in any event be no less favorable than the definition accorded any third party.

4. "PASSIVE" PAYMENTS

(a) If the Picture, as released, was based on the rights granted and material written by you hereunder and if you shall receive sole writing credit in connection therewith, and provided you shall faithfully and completely keep and perform each and every covenant and condition of this Agreement on your part to be kept and performed, then for a period of five (5) years after the initial release of the Picture, if Purchaser elects, in its sole discretion, to produce or authorize the production of the initial theatrical sequel, initial theatrical remake, MOW, miniseries or TV series pilot based upon the Picture, and if you do not render writing services in connection with such theatrical remake, theatrical sequel, MOW, miniseries or TV pilot, then you shall be entitled to receive the following passive payments (reduced by one-half [1/2] for shared credit).

(i) Additional Payments: Sequel or Remake Theatrical Motion Pictures

(1) For each sequel motion picture intended for initial theatrical release which is produced by or

under the authority of Purchaser and which is based upon the Picture, you shall be paid an amount equal to one half (1/2) of the sums actually paid to you under Paragraph 2 hereof, plus an amount equal to one half (1/2) of the applicable percentage (if any) specified in Paragraph 3 hereof, of the Net Profits of such sequel.

(2) For each remake motion picture intended for initial theatrical release which is produced by or under the authority of Purchaser and which is based upon the Picture, you shall be paid an amount equal to one third (1/3) of the sums actually paid to you for the Picture under Paragraph 2, plus an amount equal to one third (1/3) of the applicable percentage (if any) specified in Paragraph 3 hereof, of the Net Profits of such remake.

(3) The fixed sums due you pursuant to this sub-paragraph (i) shall be payable upon commencement of principal photography of such sequel or remake theatrical motion picture, as the case may be.

(4) The foregoing payments for sequel or remake theatrical motion pictures shall entitle Purchaser to unlimited rights of exhibition and exploitation with respect to each such sequel or remake in perpetuity, in any and all media whether now existing or hereafter devised.

(ii) Additional Payments Television Series

For each production produced by or under the authority of Purchaser which is an episode of a television series, and which series is based upon the Picture, and which is intended for initial exhibition on free United States prime time network television, you shall be paid the following amounts (reducible by one-half (1/2) for episodes intended for initial exhibition in the United States on other than free prime-time network television), such payment for each such episode shall be made upon the broadcast of each such episode:

(1) One Thousand Two Hundred Fifty Dollars ($1,250) for each episode of not more than thirty (30) minutes in length.

(2) One Thousand Five Hundred Dollars ($1,500) for each episode of more than thirty (30) minutes but not more than sixty (60) minutes in length; and

(3) One Thousand Seven Hundred Fifty Dollars ($1,750) for each episode of more than sixty (60) minutes in length; and

(4) If any such television program is rerun, you shall be paid one hundred percent (100%) of the applicable sum initially paid you pursuant to subparagraphs (ii) (1) through (ii) (3) above spread over the second, third, fourth, fifth, and sixth runs. No further rerun payments shall be due or payable for any run after the sixth run.

(iii) Additional Payments MOW or Mini-Series

For each motion picture produced by or under the authority of Purchaser which is an MOW or mini-series, and which is based upon the Picture, and which is intended for initial exhibition in the United States on free prime time network television, you shall be paid Ten Thousand Dollars ($10,000) for each hour thereof, up to a maximum of Eighty Thousand Dollars ($80,000), reducible by one-half (1/2) if intended for initial exhibition in the United States on other than free prime-time network television. Such payment shall be made upon broadcast of the MOW or Mini-Series.

(iv) Application of Payments

The amounts payable to you under this Paragraph 4 shall be deemed an advance against and deductible from (or where allowed, in lieu of) any amounts which may become payable to you pursuant to the Writers Guild of America ("WGA") Basic Agreement ("WGA Agreement") or any other guild agreement which may be applicable, in connection with television programs, sequel or remake theatrical motion pictures, and the reverse shall also be the case. No duplication of payment or second payment under this Paragraph 4 shall be made to you in the event that the theatrical sequel or remake shall be released for television exhibition or in the event that any television program, sequel or remake shall be released theatrically.

5. Writing Services.

In consideration for the amounts payable to you hereunder, and other good and valuable consideration, the receipt and adequacy of which you hereby acknowledge, you shall perform such rewrite and polish services as may be required by Purchaser in connection with the Property from the date hereof until completion of principal photography of the Picture, if any. No additional sums shall be payable to you in connection with the writing services which may be required by Purchaser pursuant to this paragraph. All results and proceeds of your writing services hereunder are being performed for Purchaser as a work-made-for-hire, with Purchaser being deemed the sole author and copyright holder thereof throughout the universe in perpetuity.

6. RIGHTS.

(a) If the Option is exercised, you hereby assign to Purchaser, exclusively, in perpetuity and throughout the universe, all right, title and interest, including the entire copyright, in the Property, including, without limitation, all motion picture rights, all television rights (pay, free, film, tape, cassette, cable, live and otherwise) and all allied and incidental rights in the Property, including, by way of further illustration, sequel and remake rights, music rights, soundtrack album rights, merchandising rights, radio rights, stage rights and promotional and advertising rights.

(b) The rights herein granted include the right to distribute, transmit, exhibit, broadcast and otherwise exploit all works produced pursuant to the rights granted hereunder by means of any and all media and devices whether now known or hereafter devised, and in any and all markets whatsoever, as well as the right of Purchaser in its discretion to make any and all changes in, additions to and deletions from the Property, as well as the right to use, in a reasonable and customary manner, your name, likeness and biography in and in connection with the exploitation of the rights granted hereunder; provided, that in no event shall your name, likeness and/or biography be used hereunder to endorse any product, service, individual or entity, or other than in connection with the exploitation of the rights granted hereunder. Nothing contained in this Option Agreement shall be construed as requiring Purchaser to exercise or exploit any of the rights granted to Purchaser hereunder.

(c) You agree that Purchaser shall have the unlimited right to vary, change, alter, modify, add to and/or delete from all or any part of the Property (including without limitation the title or titles thereto), and to rearrange and/or transpose all or any part of the Property and change the sequence thereof and the characters and descriptions of the characters contained in the Property and to use a portion or portions of the Property in conjunction with any other literary, dramatic or other material of any kind.

7. REPRESENTATIONS AND WARRANTIES

You hereby represent and warrant that: (a) the Property and all material to be written by you hereunder (the "Revisions") is or shall be written by and shall be wholly original with you; (b) neither the Property, the Revisions nor any element thereof infringes the copyright in any other work; (c) neither the Property, the Revisions nor their exploitation will violate the rights to privacy or publicity of any person or constitute a defamation against any person, or in any other way violate the rights of any person whomsoever; (d) you own all rights optioned to Purchaser free and clear of any liens, encumbrances, and other third party interests, and any claims or litigation, whether pending or threatened; (e) you have full right and power to make and perform this Option Agreement without the consent of any third party; (f) the Property has not previously been exploited as a motion picture or television production; and (g) the Property does and will continue to enjoy either statutory or common law copyright protection in the United States and all countries adhering to either or both the Berne and Universal Copyright Conventions. You hereby agree to defend, indemnify and hold harmless Purchaser, its successors, licensees and assigns and the directors, shareholders, employees and agents of the foregoing, from and against any and all claims, damages, liabilities, costs and expenses (including reasonable attorneys' fees) arising out of the breach or alleged breach by you of any warranty or undertaking made or to be performed by you under the terms of this Option Agreement.

8. ADDITIONAL DOCUMENTS

At Purchaser's request and expense, you will execute any and all additional documents and instruments reasonably necessary or desirable to effectuate purposes of this Option Agreement (including, without limitation, short-form options and assignments in the form attached hereto and by this reference incorporated herein). You hereby irrevocably appoint Purchaser (or Purchaser's designee) as attorney-in-fact with full power to execute, acknowledge, deliver and record in the US Copyright Office or elsewhere any and all such documents which you fail to execute, acknowledge and deliver within five (5) business days after Purchaser's request therefor.

9. CREDIT

You shall receive screenplay credit on screen and in paid advertising issued by Purchaser or under its direct control in connection with the Picture as if the standards of the WGA Agreement controlled this Agreement (provided any decisions which under the WGA Agreement are to be made by the WGA or any arbitration panel shall instead be made by Purchaser in accordance with WGA standards). You shall also receive story credit on screen to be shared with _____ in size and position to be determined by Purchaser. In addition, you shall receive credit on screen as "co-producer" of the Picture in a size and position to be determined by Purchaser in its sole discretion. It is acknowledged and agreed that no casual or inadvertent failure by Purchaser to accord such credit nor the failure for any reason by third parties to comply with the pro-visions of this paragraph, shall be deemed a breach hereof by Purchaser. It is further acknowledged and agreed that neither such failure, nor any other breach of this Option Agreement, shall entitle you to equitable relief, whether injunctive or otherwise, against or with respect to the Picture or any other works produced pursuant to the rights granted hereunder or their exploitation, since your remedy of money damages at law is adequate.

10. COPYRIGHT

All rights granted and agreed to be granted to Purchaser under this Option Agreement shall be irrevocably vested in Purchaser (including, without limitation, for the full term of copyright protection everywhere in the world and any and all renewals thereof), and shall not be subject to rescission by you or any other party for any cause, nor shall said rights be subject to termination or reversion by operation of law or otherwise, except to the extent, if any, that the provisions of any copyright law or similar law relating to the right to terminate grants of, and/or recapture rights in, literary property may apply. If the rights granted to Purchaser hereunder shall revert to you pursuant to the provisions of any copyright law or similar law, and if you are at any time thereafter prepared to enter into an agreement with a third party for the license, exercise or other disposition of all or any of such rights, you shall, before entering into such agreement, give Purchaser written notice of the terms thereof and the party involved. Purchaser shall then have fourteen (14) days in which to elect to acquire the rights involved on the terms contained in the notice. If Purchaser so elects in writing, you shall enter into a written agreement with Purchaser with regard thereto.

11. FEDERAL COMMUNICATIONS ACT

You are aware that it is a criminal offense under the Federal Communications Act, as amended, for any person to accept or pay any money, service or other valuable consideration for the inclusion of any plug, reference, product identification or other matter as part of a television program, without disclosure in the manner required by law. You understand that it is the policy of Purchaser to prohibit the acceptance or payment of any such consideration, and you represent that you have not accepted or paid and agree that you shall not accept or pay any such consideration.

12. ASSIGNMENT

Purchaser shall have the right to assign any or all of its rights under this Option Agreement to any person, and any such assignment shall relieve Purchaser of its obligations to you under this Option Agreement, provided that such assignee assumes all of Purchaser's obligations hereunder in writing. You shall not have the right to assign this Option Agreement.

13. FORCE MAJEURE

The option period hereunder shall be subject to extension for any period of default and/or force majeure (including without limitation any strike by any guild, union or other labor organization against motion picture producers during the option period) if said force majeure event materially inhibits Purchaser's ability to develop the Property, and any period during which any claim remains outstanding or unresolved which involves the breach or alleged breach of any of your warranties, representations or agreements herein.

14. APPLICABLE LAW/JURISDICTION

This Agreement will be interpreted in accordance with the laws of the State of California applicable to agreements entered into and to be wholly performed therein. You hereby consent to the exclusive jurisdiction of the courts (State and Federal) located in the County of Los Angeles, State of California.

15. NOTICES

(a) All notices from Purchaser to you shall be sent to you at the address on page one hereof.

(b) All notices from you to Purchaser shall be sent to Purchaser at the address on page one hereof with a mandatory copy to:

_____

_____

_____

(c) All payments which Purchaser may be required to make to you hereunder shall be delivered or sent to you by mail or telegraph at the address for payments set forth on page one hereof, and you acknowledge that payment in such fashion shall be a good and valid discharge of all such indebtedness to you.

16. RENTAL RIGHT

You acknowledge and agree that the following sums are in consideration of, and constitute equitable remuneration for, the rental right included in the rights granted hereunder: (1) an agreed allocation to the rental right of 3.8% of the fixed compensation and, if applicable, 3.8% of the contingent compensation provided for in this Agreement; and (2) any sums payable to you with respect to the rental right under any applicable collective bargaining or other industry-wide agreement; and (3) the residuals payable to you under any such collective bargaining or industry-wide agreement with respect to home video exploitation which are reasonably attributable to sale of home video devices for rental purposes in the territories or jurisdictions where the rental right is recognized. If under the applicable law of any territory or jurisdiction, any additional or different form of compensation is required to satisfy the requirement of equitable remuneration, then it is agreed that the grant to Purchaser of the rental right shall nevertheless be fully effective, and Purchaser shall pay you such compensation or, if necessary, the parties shall in good faith negotiate the amount and nature thereof in accordance with applicable law. Since Purchaser has already paid or agreed to pay you equitable remuneration for the rental right, you hereby assign to Purchaser, except to the extent specifically reserved to you under any applicable collective bargaining or other industry-wide agreement, all compensation for the rental right payable or which may become payable to you on account or in the nature of a tax or levy, through a collecting society or otherwise. You shall cooperate fully with Purchaser in the collection and payment to Purchaser of such compensation. Further, since under this Agreement Purchaser has already paid or agreed to pay you full consideration for all rights granted by you hereunder, you hereby assign to Purchaser, except to the extent specifically reserved to you under any applicable collective bargaining or other industry-wide agreement, all other compensation payable or which may become payable to you on account or in the nature of a tax or levy, through a collecting society or otherwise, under the applicable law of any territory or jurisdiction, including by way of illustration only, so-called blank tape and similar levies. You shall cooperate fully with Purchaser in connection with the collection and payment to Purchaser of all such compensation.

17. IMMIGRATION REFORM ACT

You warrant and represent that you are eligible to be employed in the United States in compliance with the Immigration Reform Act of 1986, as amended. As a condition precedent to your receipt of any payment hereunder, you will complete the requisite I-9 Form and will present such form to Purchaser along with the requisite documentation, as specified on the I-9 Form, evidencing that you may be lawfully employed.

18. CONFLICT WAIVER

The parties hereto acknowledge that the law firm of_____
("Firm") has heretofore been retained by each of them as attorneys-at-law to furnish each of them legal advice and services, including with respect to the Property and this Agreement. The parties further acknowledge that, at their joint request, the Firm has drafted this letter agreement, which is intended to memorialize the agreement between the parties. We acknowledge that the Firm's joint representation of us has been with the knowledge, informed consent and approval of each of us, and we will not assert any claim at any time that the agreement is not valid because of such representation. We further acknowledge that we have been advised to seek, and have had ample opportunity to seek, independent business and legal counseling with respect to such representation and this Agreement.

19. ENTIRE UNDERSTANDING

This Agreement constitutes the entire understanding between the parties and cannot be modified except by written agreement signed by Purchaser and you.

20. MISCELLANEOUS

If there is any conflict between any provisions of this Option Agreement and any present or future statute, law, ordinance or regulation, the latter shall prevail; provided, that the provision hereof so affected shall be limited only to the extent necessary and no other provision shall be affected.

Please signify your agreement to the foregoing by signing this letter in the space provided below.

Very truly yours,

_____

By: _____

Its: _____

AGREED TO AND ACCEPTED:

_____
_____
_____
_____

. . .

THE STORY MERCHANT

TITLE:	COVERAGE BY:
Qumran	▮▮▮▮▮▮
AUTHOR:	**DATE RECEIVED:**
Jerry Amernic	6/30/2014
TYPE:	**DATE COMPLETED:**
Manuscript	7/8/2014
SCORE: **RECOMMEND,** w/development	
PAGES:	**GENRE(S):**
325	Adventure, Historical thriller

LOGLINE:

Archeologist David Marr finds the mummified remains of a 2000 year old crucified man outside Jerusalem at the ruins of Qumran. Various religious sects descend upon David to use his discovery for their own aims.

SYNOPSIS:

David Marr is an archeologist and professor at the Hebrew University in Jerusalem. During a weekend dig in the ruins of Qumar, with his student assistant Robbie Schueftan, they discover a mummy buried in the sand. After sneaking the mummy back into his lab at the university Professor Marr does a series of tests. These tests show the mummy is easily 2000 years old and has been crucified.

Looking for a second opinion in what he has found he contacts his oldest friend and colleague, Jamil Hassad, head of pathological science at the University of Alexandria. Jamil does a series of rigorous tests on the mummy. When David asks him about his findings Jamil goes pale and begins praying to Allah. He warns David of his discovery, telling him he should bury it back in the desert. David does not heed Jamil and expresses his intentions to keep studying the mummy. Jamil alludes that David may have found the remains of Jesus Christ and warns him of the violent and long lasting effects a discovery such as this could have on the Holy Land. He tells David not to let anyone know about the mummy; David agrees. Jamil is forced to return to Egypt on business but vows to return and aid in David's continued study of the mummy.

David begins having trouble hiding his discovery. Eliraz Shimron another professor at the University consistently tries to get David to show her what he found. Even going so far as to try and seduce him.

As David continues his studies we begin to learn more about his past. It is revealed that when he was a very young archeology student studying in Jerusalem he had a hand in discovering the Dead Sea Scrolls and researching the Essenes who were hypothesized to have written the scrolls. He witnessed his mentor Professor Solnik being ridiculed by the press for discovering and interpreting the Dead Sea Scrolls in a way that went against preconceived religious dogma. David also begins romancing Gita Levitt during his time in Jerusalem; this woman would eventually become his wife.

Back in the present David continues having trouble trying to dodge Eliraz's constant questioning. He decides to let her help him in his research while keeping out significant details. He gives her blood from the mummy to test and they discover that the mummy had sickle cell anaemia.

David is then called back to the ruins at Qumran where they discover another body buried in the desert. However this is not a mummy but instead a decapitated skeleton. Robbie and the Professor hypothesize these are the remains of John the Baptist. They take the skeleton back to the lab and Robbie expresses his fear of the mummy and skeleton and asks Professor Marr to return them to the desert, he once again refuses.

We learn more about Marr's history as an archaeologist and his run in with what was supposedly the Holy Grail. While visiting England with his wife, son Brian, and daughter Jenni, the family goes to a monastery that boasts to house the real holy grail in its catacombs. David impresses one of the monks with his knowledge of history and asks if he can see the grail. The monk warns that what they have is a fake with a curse on it. Whoever touches the grail in the catacombs usually befalls a calamity dealing with children. David however is a man of science and is taken to where the grail is. He examines it and deems it a fake. Sometime later David's daughter is diagnosed with diabetes, and his son dies in an accident during an archaeological dig in Jerusalem. The idea that David's curiosity could have been the reason his children met such cruel fates still haunts him.

David gives another blood sample to test, this time from The Shroud of Turin, which he acquired while studying it in Italy. Although David deemed the shroud a fake, the blood from the shroud, and the blood from the mummy come back as an exact match. He phones Jamil who agrees to return to Jerusalem and help David further study the mummy. He also phones Gita who comes to the Holy Land to help her husband.

We learn of David's time on a committee studying the Shroud of Turin. He deemed it a well done forgery and nothing more but caught a lot of resistance from other scientists who were obviously bought off by the church. He also stole a small fragment from The Shroud to study himself. He was almost caught by Cardinal Fiori, a man who put a strange and unnerving feeling in David.

Eliraz goes missing from the school but not before getting drunk and revealing some of the information about David's discovery to a reporter at a party. This creates a huge problem for David as now the press constantly hounds him demanding to know what he found. This also brings unwanted attention from Muslim and Jewish radical groups who start employing spies and thieves to try and break into David's lab.

Before arriving in Jerusalem, Gita stops in Rome and visits the Vatican Library hoping to find something that would help David. She finds a book which leads her and David back to Qumran where they find another Dead Sea Scroll. However her visit to the library was discovered and tracked by Cardinal Fiori, so now even the Catholic Church turns its powerful gaze towards David.

Back in Jerusalem, David goes to visit Eliraz who has returned after disappearing for a few weeks. She informs David that she has quit working at the University and decided to teach underprivileged Palestinians in the refugee camps outside of Jerusalem. David goes to meet her one day for lunch and witnesses her death in a mass suicide bombing.

Realizing the danger he has put his friends and family in he returns to Qumran with Gita. They find the final Dead Sea Scrolls with instructions on how to bury two very important members in the desert. This strengthens David's hypothesis that Jesus and John the Baptist were members of the Essenes community in Qumran. However David is unable to use this discovery as he and his wife are captured by Israeli fundamentalists who demand he hand over the scroll at gunpoint. David begrudgingly does so and the scroll is lost.

Jamil returns and helps David perform a CAT scan on the mummy. One night while working on the mummy an armed Muslim breaks into the lab. Jamil engages in a violent hand to hand fight with the man, which ends in his death. Jamil and David use chemicals to make the body appear as if it were a very old mummy and hide it in the university's morgue.

David is finally contacted by the Catholic Church who demand he hand over what he discovered. David, Jamil, Robbie, and Gita meet none other than Cardinal Fiori in the desert. They give him a mummy but it is in fact the man Jamil killed days ago made to look like a mummified crucified corpse. David and the Cardinal walk around the ruins of Qumran one last time. Fiori expresses his desire to have the ruins bulldozed along with anything else contradicting the church's rule. After a tense moment the Cardinal and his subordinates take the body with them.

David goes back to his lab with Robbie and they return the mummy they found and the skeleton to the desert where they found them. They bury the corpses deep so that no one can find them. David finally realizing this was the right thing to do as a discovery like this would do nothing to help the violent climate in the Holy Land.

Gita informs David that she took up Eliraz's old job of teaching Palestinian refugees. He goes to her class and is happy to see her making a difference. He drives out to the Dead Sea and feels the spirit of his son, the mummy he found, and something more having a moment of religious relief he has finally found some sense of peace.

OVERALL:

This is a very interesting work of fiction that ties in a lot of real world archeology, theology, and political events into a very satisfying thriller. At its bests it shines in its ability to make drier more scientific concepts easy to understand and very entertaining. The cast of characters are all very interesting, and each one has an arc with satisfying growth. I would like to see more plot elements better fleshed out, some character development seems rushed, and there were some pacing issues I felt slowed the plot down quite a bit. However I thoroughly enjoyed the story this book aimed to tell, and could see it being popular with many readers.

STRUCTURE:

Events unfolded very succinctly in this manuscript. It did a good job of giving you enough answers as to not feel fully in the dark but at the same time raising enough questions to keep one reading and fully engaged in the plot. I liked how every section of the book would be punctuated by a flashback where we would learn more about David's life, his work, and his family. However sometimes there would be sections of pure textbook information about archeology, history, and science and I would like to see these areas better incorporated into the plot. As they are now they slow pacing down. This could be remedied by having David explain these concepts in class or in conversation with others to make the information seem more engaging.

CONFLICT:

I enjoyed the overarching conflict of this discovery being dangerous to the world and trying to hide it until David had all the information he wanted. I also enjoyed that they never out right say they believe the mummy they have are the remains of Jesus Christ. It keeps the reader guessing and heightens the tensions in the early parts of the book. However I felt in the final third of the book the actions really started ramping up out of nowhere. It wasn't really a slow build to the boiling point as it seemed to ramp up out of the blue. I think elements of the Jewish extremists could have been introduced earlier in the book to add another element of danger that has a slow rise. As it is now I felt that the extremists, the reporters, and the church all come in at the end to bring the tension to a high and then become quickly wrapped up. I think introducing these elements earlier and letting them slowly increase in intensity over the course of the entire novel would be more beneficial to a story like this. It would also keep the reader more engaged in some of the drier areas where it slows down.

CHARACTER:

All of the characters were interesting and their interactions with each other were well done and felt very dynamic. However I would have liked to see more of the supporting characters, namely Robbie, Eliraz, and Gita. Robbie is the Professor's protégé but disappears in certain sections of the book particularly the middle and end. It's not really mentioned where he is or what he is doing. He's an interesting character and seems to be the most neutral of all the characters in the book and his personal insight is interesting in every scene he is in. I would have liked to see him incorporated more into the book. At times he just seems to be there as a comic relief element or as a stand in to ask questions that would allow David to explain scientific and archeological terms and history. Eliraz was another very interesting character that felt underutilized. It was also never fully clear to me why she decided to leave the school and teach at the refugee camp. Her arc feels very rushed and without warrant. Playing her up more as an antagonist in the beginning and then slowly making her into a more sympathetic character seems to be the author's intent, but she needs to be in more scenes in order for the reader to get attached to her the way the author intends. Finally Gita should also be more present from the beginning of the novel. I don't think she begins to turn up until almost halfway through the book. Her development at the end is also very rushed and without almost any reason. She goes from a very proud Jew who believes her way and her people are the only thing that matters to a very understanding and accepting person. Going so far as to express her new beliefs takes, "A little from every religion." This sudden change in her character is very jarring and it doesn't feel earned by the end of the book. Having her more present in the beginning could help the reader understand and then show how the death of her children affected her. Thus further mapping out the change in her character. She also is not very likable when described from the doctor's perspective, so more scenes with her may help her develop in a softer light. Overall I enjoyed the characters in this story and their individual arcs but at the end felt like I'd missed a section that would have made all their development come full circle.

DIALOGUE:

I enjoyed the use of dialogue in this piece. Mixing the various languages of the region into conversation to illustrate how diverse the mix of cultures in the Holy Land is. I also liked how there was often no translation for the instances of foreign language to make the reader feel like David in his confusion and inability to fully understand the region. I also enjoyed David's clever banter as well as Robbie never using contractions or idioms. Each character's dialogue felt very unique to them and made them truly come alive. All the characters had their own voice that helped make the world of the book seem real and plausible. Very few of the lines felt like filler and every conversation seemed to have an underlying motive that kept it very engaging.

PACING:

As mentioned before I felt this manuscript did a great job of giving enough information and adding more questions to keep the reader engaged. For the most part I also enjoyed how flashbacks to David's life were peppered throughout the narrative but at times this seemed to detract from the conflict. Especially the long section where it goes over how David worked his way into the group of scientists studying the Shroud of Turin. There was a lot of exposition that lacked tension and boiled down to someone telling David he needed to be in a certain society or guild of scientists to be accepted into the group of scientists that were studying and then he simply joins it with little effort. This specific flashback was too long and detracted from the overall conflict and slowed the pace of the story down quite a bit and I don't think the pacing fully recovers until near the end of the manuscript. Portions of the Shroud of Turin flashback can be omitted as I do not think they are pertinent to the story. Furthermore there are a few sections of pure textbook exposition expounding upon ideas, histories, scientific concepts, and archeological studies that come off as very dry and slow the overall pace of the piece. For example in the beginning right after discovering the mummy David begins talking about other mummies found around the world that were fakes or had changed the modern understanding of the ancient world significantly. I can see how these are pertinent to the story but this exposition comes up before a conflict is even established. This information is important but I think it should be discussed after the main conflict has been established, maybe instead of straight explanation this information could be delivered through dialogue or in a way that feels more organic to the narrative.

LOGIC:

The work relies on the reader's understanding of archeology, the scientific process, religious history, as well as socio-political ideologies of the Holy Lands. The author does a remarkable job of introducing all these elements and giving the reader a great understanding of them, without being boring or heavy handed. However some of the decisions the characters made (Eliraz going to teach in the refugee camp, Gita deciding to do the same, Robbie going to the dangerous meeting with the Cardinal in the desert) seemed odd or a bit of a jump of the believable side. However this could easily be solved by more scenes with those characters to further develop them. Also when David and Gita lose the final Dead Sea Scroll to the Jewish radical that plot point drops off and it isn't really discussed or mentioned again. The skeleton of John the Baptist is also another loose hanging plot thread that could have used further elaboration. The lack of consistency and resolution in these minor conflicts chips a well-polished story. More time could be devoted to these conflicts or they could be cut out of the story completely and I don't see their loss detracting from the narrative in any way.

CRAFT:

The descriptive writing in this piece is very well done. It shows a deep understanding of the area and of archeology. It paints a perfect picture of the Holy Land and I think the craft is where this piece really shines.

POTENTIAL FOR FILM (if applicable):

Although this is a manuscript I could see a story like this being streamlined into a very good film or miniseries. It has enough mystery, action, and suspense while also being topical and interesting to a wide range of viewers. I think overall with a few minor issues in the pacing and minor conflicts that could use further development this could be a very strong work in the visual medium.

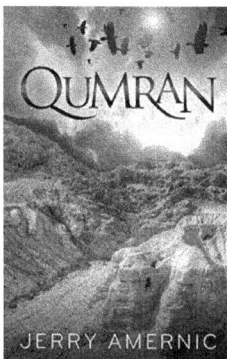

QUMRAN

JERRY AMERNIC

Ed. Note: *This coverage led us to publish the novel, and to pursue film possibilities for it. The book by Jerry Amernic can be purchased at*

Story Merchant:

http://www.ama-zon.com/dp/B00VQPBKCK/?tag=stormerc-20

or

Amazon:

http://amzn.com/B00VQPBKCK

13 Rules for Breaking into "the Business"

from *A Writer's Time: Making the Time to Write (Revised and Expanded);* e-book: *Write: Time*

1. *Visualize your success.* It really does help to see yourself in the auditorium waiting to hear if you've won the Emmy you've been nominated for, or holding a check from that major studio in your hand for the first time. These things happen and they tend to happen sooner to writers who foresee them. It's a great motivator!

2. *Take full responsibility for your career.* No matter how many agents, managers, or attorneys you work with never forget that you're the quarterback of your team and it's your creativity that put the team together and your decision that will direct the team's future. Take advice from those you trust and respect, but follow your own gut.

3. *Know your market.* The more you know about the business you're in, the more success you'll have in it. Success isn't necessarily solely financial; it's also acceptance, and the satisfaction of knowing that when you say you have a new story people you know will call you back to hear about it.

4. *Be willing to learn the hard way.* Although there's almost nothing easy in show business, that's a

good thing, right? What better than a career built on challenges, one in which you'll never stop learning and growing as you move forward? Doing is a better way of learning than thinking or studying.

5. *Don't be afraid to trust people.* Even though "these people are not your friends," they *are* driven professionals who operate most responsibly when they're trusted by those who work with them. If something shakes your trust in someone, confront it immediately; you'll learn that most of the time it was caused by lack of communication or of understanding.

6. *Reject rejection.* Toughen up when it comes to negatives. Don't think of passes as negatives, but as "one more wrong person" who's not going to endanger my vision by making the movie.

7. *Honor thy contacts.* Contacts in Hollywood are hard to come by, so once you have them, take care of them. Keep in touch, without being obtrusive. Keep an eye on their progress, and congratulate them when you see them do something cool. They will remember you when the time comes for you to approach them. And *don't approach them* until you have something terrific.

8. *Stay off everyone's "life is too short" list.* Brilliant writers fail because they're obnoxious. Brilliance doesn't entitle you to be unbearable,

massively self-centered, or unappreciative. If you insist on being that way you'll find yourself on that LITS list for sure: "No matter how wonderful his stories are I'd rather not work with him or her. Life is too short."

9. *Think big.* There are fewer people thinking big, and in Hollywood it's *not* that exciting to hear "it's a small little picture that can be done for a budget." Money is rarely an issue with Hollywood film budgets. The more that's needed, the easier it is to raise it—assuming the story is wonderful and BIG.

10. *Don't forget to take* vacations *regularly.* Sometimes you'll believe you're depressed by the effort you're putting in, especially when compared to the results you're seeing. Make sure you're not confusing depression with *exhaustion.* This *is* an exhausting career you've chosen. Give yourself frequent breaks, the longer, the more you need it: a night out with the boys or girls, a weekend out of town, a week or two in Naples. You'll see that when you're away a time will come when you can't *wait* to be back at your desk. That is a good thing, a thing to plan for.

11. *Avoid "future greed."* When you finally get a deal, and decide it's time life paid you back for all your previous suffering, don't put that burden on a single deal, especially not on your *first* deal.

12. *Lighten up.* Some writers take the whole thing so seriously I get nervous watching their faces redden as their blood pressure goes up. Consider that on the universal scale of things, you are just one of a history of writers trying to work your trade. Whatever you do will have no effect on Centauri b. Keep your perspective toward your career, and take *it* seriously, not *yourself.*

13. *Celebrate each step along the rocky road.* Make it a rule that you'll celebrate *every good step* you take, whether it's a relatively small one like sending in your first script to a manager who wants to read it or a huge one like walking onto the set of *your* first film. You've chosen this most challenging of careers, and you *deserve* to celebrate just for sticking to your choice.

HOLLYWOOD
JARGON

Acquisition editors: The executives at a traditional publishing house who read incoming manuscripts and announce the decision of whether they will be accepted or rejected.

Acquisition meeting: Usually held on Monday morning, the meeting where Hollywood story editors pitch the executives on stories they've rated as "recommend" and answer queries, if any, about stories they are *not* recommending.

Acts: Drama, of which film is a most prodigious subset, has a beginning, middle, and end that are loosely known as "acts." Although the three-act structure has been around since the classical Greeks, the number of acts can also be four (preferred, for example, by Todd Klick's *Beat by Beat*) or even seven (used by television movies). What's happening in these variances is that act two, which I refer to in one of my books as the "Serengeti Plain" because it punishes so many dramatists with its seemingly interminable length compared to act one and the final act, is simply being divided to make it easier to conquer. In other words, in a network film, act two is divided into act two, act three, act four, act five, and act six, leaving act seven to bring us a satisfying conclusion.

Back end: When all the expenses associated with a film have been paid off and the investors recouped, we've reached the back end. Which is where "profits" come in.

Beat sheet: A writing tool used to identify the sequence of events and actions in your story. It is an abbreviated way to break down the structure of your story, making it easier to organize and change. The beat sheet charts the sequence of events that cause your main character to do something and maps how your main character changes from the beginning to the end of your story. Create a beat sheet by using bullet points that illustrate in one or two lines the order of your plot's progression. Remember plot takes place when a character does something or acts upon another character.

Character arc: How a character changes from beginning to end is called the "arc." With a minor character, it can take as few as three scenes to define them. A major character makes slower progress along his or her arc.

Climax: The final act of a screenplay weaves all threads of its dramatic action together in a climax that brings the story to a satisfying conclusion.

Compensated: Compensation, i.e., being *paid,* comes in two forms: front-end, a payment that occurs upon either signing a contract or upon the start of filming, or both; and back-end, which includes both "contingent compensation," covering what happens if your film leads to a sequel or prequel, a television series, or a remake—and profit participation, which gives you a share in the producer's revenues from the film.

Completion bond: A financial agreement from a guarantor that he will assume the responsibility for completing the film on budget and on time. Though the bonding company works hand in hand with the producers and director, it holds the absolute power to take over the filming if necessary, to accomplish that goal. The takeover rarely has to happen.

Contingent compensation: Your negotiated share of the profits of a film.

Creative dialogue: The interaction between producers, actors, director and the screenwriter in which notes are proposed, discussed, and either implemented or put aside.

Credit: If you're a writer, your "credit" on a film is determined only by the Writers Guild of America's accreditation committee. In Hollywood, credits are as important as money so make sure you've got a good attorney who will fight for the credit you deserve.

Development Hell: When a film languishes at a studio or production company and has yet to reach the day of principal photography (the first day of shooting), and that's gone on for a year or more, you're officially in development hell. One of our films had four sets of writers involved, four directors, two stars, and still hasn't made it to the screen…yet.

Domestic distributor: A film distributor who places your finished film in theaters, or releases it to television, or in both markets, in the United States and Canada.

Equity: A term that in most businesses means a risk investment of actual capital into a project that has no guaranteed certainty of breaking even. In the film business, equity is structured as a loan to the film, repayable plus a fixed rate, from revenues.

Film stock: The physical blank film upon which the camera creates images during filmmaking. Since films often don't use a portion of a reel of film, extra film is sometimes available for postproduction facilities to sell or donate.

Fixed compensation: The contractual amount paid for the dramatic rights to an underlying intellectual property (I.P.), as opposed to "contingent compensation." The I.P. contracted for includes the script and every preceding form of the story it is based on or inspired by.

Franchise: An established brand, like the Bond movies, *Spiderman,* or Ripley's Believe-It-or-Not!

Genre: A "category" or "kind" of story, like dramatic romance, romantic comedy, action, action-adventure, epic, sci-fi, etc.

Going wide: An expression that means the person who's selling your story is submitting it to many buyers at once, instead of using the selective approach.

Hollywood: "Hollywood" has long ago become the metaphorical word for referring to the entertainment business mostly centered in greater Los Angeles—ranging from Santa Monica to Burbank, from Beverly Hills to Valencia, but not really in Hollywood-proper. The actual Hollywood, where Hollywood Boulevard is, is where you find the tourist attraction Grauman's Chinese Theater as well as the Hollywood sign and the Dolby Theater where the Academy Awards presentation takes place.

Intensity rating: A graph presented in *Writing Treatments That Sell* that charts the rise and fall of action in a story on a scene-by-scene basis.

I.P.: Short for "intellectual property," the legal term describing any kind of story material created by an author and transmitted by legal contract to a buyer who intends to make a motion picture or television program based on it.

Logline: A one-line pitch of your story, very much like the one-liners you would read in *TV Guide*. Also known as an "elevator pitch," or "one-liner."

Marketing array: Various forms of the pitch for your story: treatment, logline, one-paragraph, etc.

MBA: Minimum Basic Agreement, of the Writers Guild of America.

Obligatory action or scenes: The actions or scenes in a story that *must be physically shown* for the story to make sense.

Option price: The price paid to a holder of underlying rights (treatment, book, screenplay, etc.) to allow the buyer a specified amount of time to set up all the elements required for the movie to be made.

Option-purchase agreement: The standard agreement by which a buyer acquires control over an I.P. by optioning it for a certain price for a certain period of time, with a promise to purchase it by a certain date—or return all rights back to the creator.

Participation: Your share of the profits of a motion picture.

Pitch: A description of a story, intended to sell the listener on it immediately. A pitch can be oral or written.

Postproduction: The filmmaking phase that begins the last day of principal photography, and sometimes even earlier, in which the film is edited, sound and visual effects and music added, and all mixed with the images until the film is finalized.

Preempt: A preemptive bid, preempt for short, is a bid whose intention is to take the story off the market immediately and is therefore accompanied by a short deadline for response. For example, a studio will make an offer and give the seller's representative a few hours to respond to it before removing the offer from the table.

Premise: The one sentence that encapsulates an entire story and permeates its every scene: "Overwhelming ambition leads to self-destruction" (see Lajos Egri, *The Art of Dramatic Writing*).

Prep: Short for "preproduction," the period before the actual filming of a movie begins, during which all facets of the production are brought to readiness for the filming.

Pre-sold audience: A film project that can claim it's already a household name, like the many Marvel comics or *The Lord of the Rings*.

Principal photography: The day when the film begins shooting; when the cameras first roll.

Protagonist: The "first actor" in a drama, often erroneously called the hero. He is the prime cause of the action that unfolds, and the story is *about him.*

Purchase price: The price paid to a creator or holder of underlying rights, usually upon the first day of principal photography, to transfer all rights from the creator/holder to the buyer, thereby protecting the buyer's investment in the film.

Query: The industry term for an inquiry, most often by email, asking the person you've emailed if they are interested in your story.

Rhythmic development: The rise and fall of dramatic action in a manner that keeps the audience fully engaged from beginning to end of a screenplay, especially in act two. Often referred to as "rising and falling action."

Set up: Usually means arranging for the financing of a motion picture, though it also refers to preparing a scene to be shot and to the establishment of all dramatic elements in act one of a screenplay.

Scene: The unit of drama, as the letters of the alphabet are the units of writing.

Spec: A shorthand for "speculation," usually referring to work done without compensation but on the hopes that it will lead to compensation, as in a "spec script."

Star: A charismatic and box-office-successful actor whose mere involvement in a film gets it financed and draws audiences to the box office.

Start date: The day on which everyone involved in the actual filming of the story is available to begin that crucial work. Start date usually refers to the commencement of preproduction.

Story editor: The title given to industry readers, who read stories for their executive, agent, manager, producer, and director bosses and report the story's potential and its flaws.

Sympathetic: The word comes originally from ancient Greek, where it means "to suffer along with" someone. Can we relate to him or her? If we can, he or she is a "sympathetic" character in our story.

Syntax: Grammatical, logical, and expository rules that govern formal prose. Drama is known for shattering syntax with surprise, power, and unexpected turns and twists as when King Lear shouts:

When we are born, we cry that we are come

To this great stage of fools. This a good block.

It were a delicate stratagem to shoe

A troop of horse with felt. I'll put 't in proof.

And when I have stol'n upon these sons-in-law,

Then, kill, kill, kill, kill, kill, kill!

Taking it out to the town: An expression that means the person who's selling your story is now ready to send it to buyers or creative allies.

Trackers: Independent contractors who hunt down those who control the rights to a given story, and report the information to their bosses (studios, production companies, directors, etc.).

Treatment: A relatively brief, loosely narrative, written pitch of a story intended for production as a film for theatrical exhibition or television broadcast. Written in user-friendly, dramatic but straightforward and highly visual prose in the present tense, the treatment highlights in broad strokes your story's hook, primary characters, acts and action line, setting, point of view, and most dramatic scenes and turning points.

Ulmer Scale: A survey that ranks on a scale of 1 to 100 the influence of more than 1,400 actors worldwide to generate movie financing. Created in 1998 by entertainment journalist James Ulmer, the survey canvases sources that range from producers, entertainment agents and studio executives to international distributors, foreign sales agents and investment bankers.

Taken into account are an actor's box office numbers, versatility, professionalism and willingness to promote films.

Underlying Rights; Underlying Property; Underlying Material: Legal terminology for the story you created in every format in which it exists (book, pitch, and/or treatment), which is intellectual property owned by you until you sell it or make your own film based on it.

On set of *Angels in the Snow*

Story Merchant Dr. Ken Atchity (Georgetown A.B., Yale PhD) has made over one hundred film and television deals for storytellers wanting their books to be films—including movies, series, and reality shows—since he began producing in 1986 after retiring his tenured professorship. Check the Internet Movie Database for a full list of his film and television credits:

http://www.imdb.com/find?ref_=nv_sr_fn&q=
Kenneth+Atchity&s=all

He's also launched hundreds of books for clients, including Wendy Eckel's mystery series at Thomas Dunne; Gerald Blaine and Lisa McCubbin's New York Times bestseller *The Kennedy Detail*, Clint Hill and Lisa McCubbin's *Mrs. Kennedy and Me* and *5 Days in November*; Dacre

Stoker and Ian Holt's *Dracula: The Un-Dead* (also NYT Bestseller); and NYT bestsellers by Governor Jesse Ventura, *I Ain't Got Time to Bleed: Reworking the Body Politic from the Bottom Up* and *Do I Stand Alone?*; Steve Alten's (the *Meg* series); and James Michael Pratt's *The Last Valentine. The Kennedy Detail* (Discovery; Emmy-nominated), *The Lost Valentine* (Hallmark Hall of Fame), and *Meg* (Warner Brothers) have been made into films along with over thirty other films Ken has produced for television and theatre.

Among over twenty books of his own, Ken's recent novels include *Seven Ways to Die* (with William Diehl; rave review from CNN's Nancy Grace), *The Messiah Matrix,* and *Brae Mackenzie.* Ken's *A Writer's Time: A Guide to the Creative Process, from Vision through Revision* (e-book: *Write: Time*) was called by the New York Times, "the best…book on writing." *Writing Treatments That Sell: How to Create and Market Your Story Ideas to the Motion Picture and TV Industry* (e-book: *Write: Treatments That Sell),* written with Chi-Li Wong, is now in its third edition.

His scripts, in various stages of development, include *Raptor,* based on Jock Miller's *Fossil River; Re-Product,* with Tokyo's Wonderium (http://www.wonderium.com); and *Andrew Jackson: Battle for New Orleans* (with Mike Maples).

Currently he's focusing his producing efforts on projects developed with writer-partners, including

Dr. Warren Woodruff's *Dr. Fuddle and the Gold Baton*, Leslie Neilan's *The Book of Leah*, and Ed Raarup's *Firefly: The Tail of Enzo.*

Ken's books include (right click to open hyperlink):

Write: Time **and** *A Writer's Time*

Write: Treatments **and** *Writing Treatments that Sell*

How to Publish Your Novel

Quit Your Day Job and Live Out Your Dreams

Seven Ways to Die **(with William Diehl)**

The Messiah Matrix

AUTHOR'S NOTE

I hope you found this little book helpful to your film ambitions. I plan to update it at least once a year. So you won't have to buy it each time, here's a proposal for you: if you review it for Amazon, and email me a copy of your review once it's posted, I'll automatically send you the first revision. I want to hear your suggestions for the next version—so please include them in your email (not your review).

I can be reached at atchity@storymerchant.com. And check out my three companies serving writers:

www.storymerchant.com
www.storymerchantbooks.com
www.thewriterslifeline.com

Please also visit www.kenatchity.blogspot.com to keep abreast of what we're up to.

I'm grateful to all the colleagues who've contributed to these observations along the way, and especially to former AEI Exec VP Mike Kuciak for his thoughts on loglines, AEI partner Chi-Li Wong for her fierce editing and helpful suggestions, Story Merchant Exec VP Lisa Cerasoli for her passion, insight and clarity, Atchity Productions Exec Director Chelsea Mongird for her constant attention to detail, our literary interns Kirsten Volkert, Christopher Kuhne, and Kevin

Theal, and Story Merchant Books Director of Design Danielle Canfield for careful proofreading.

Thank you for taking the time to read, and best of luck with your film career.

Finally, if you want to *hear* this material, please join our *Sell Your Story to Hollywood* training at
http://realfasthollywooddeal.com/

SELL YOUR

STORY

HOLLYWOOD